A SURVIVAL GUIDE FOR TEENAGERS AND PARENTS

CHALLENGE TO EXCELLENCE

Be the Best You Can Be

KATHLEEN SHEA

ILLUSTRATIONS BY DIANE DECOITE

ISBN: 9798218142537

Printed in the United States of America.

Cover and Interior design by FormattedBooks

CONTENTS

Please go to my website kathleen-shea.com
to make extra copies of handouts and worksheets.

PROLOGUE

During my early years of teaching *Challenge to Excellence*, I thought of myself as a Youth Advocate. Now, after our boys are grown and are wonderful husbands and amazing dads, my husband and I say that as parents they have "kicked it up a notch"!

I now see myself as a Family Advocate.

At the end of this book, I will tell you about the joy we feel at our family reunions with our five beautiful grandchildren and with our sons. May 30, 2023, this past Memorial Day, our joy was shattered when our youngest son, Peter Ryan had a freak surfing accident and died on Short Sands Beach in Oregon, leaving behind him his soulmate wife, Melanie and their two children: his 14-year-old son, Brogan and 11-year-old daughter, Sierra.

I would never wish this devasting grief and sadness on anyone. There is a hole in our hearts that will never heal.

Peter Ryan was/is the BEST of the Sheas.

I'm writing this Prologue for three reasons:

1. When you read Peter's "story" in Chapter Three, I want you to know that Peter was full of self-confidence. He didn't care what anyone thought about him because he knew that he was worthy—a child of God, unique, rare, valuable, a Priceless, Precious Angel. The day when he saw a classmate crying on the steps and everyone else walking by him—probably because they were worried about what others would think of them if they stopped—Peter Ryan stopped and that made all the difference in that boy's life.

2. His story is the basis of why I wrote this book. What I want for every reader is that each of you attains that same exceptional self-confidence when you grasp the value of realizing your own magnificence.

3. Family is the most important thing in the world. This book is a Family Communication Workbook. My hope is that you will use these principles during these teen years to create wonderful family memories and build unbreakable bonds that will last forever.

You only need one book for your family because you can go to my website: kathleen-shea.com, click on *MENU* go to *WORKSHEETS* and make all the copies of worksheets and handouts that you need for your family. This book is also available to listen to on Audible.

On my website you can also click on *MENU* "The Death of our Son" and click on the link to: The Grom Father Memorial Foundation if you want to learn more about Peter Ryan. You'll understand why 300 people came to his Mass and Reception and the incredible inspirational impact he had on everyone he met.

Our sons have started this Foundation to benefit Melanie, Brogan and Sierra and help other young families who have lost parents.

Pray for us.

Colorado Skiing trip - 2022

Mexico surfing trip - 2022

Loved to fly fish - 2023

Last photo of "The Five Sheas" - 2022

ACKNOWLEDGMENTS

It took a team to make my dream of publishing a book come true.

I could not have accomplished it without the talents and support of many others.

My illustrator, Diane DeCoite for enlivening the content with her exceptional drawings.

I wrote and taught Challenge to Excellence but when it came to putting into book form, that was a whole new domain and I needed help! I am indebted to Jesse at Fiverr for his editing expertise, great suggestions, insights, and feedback. He made me a better writer.

Kryssha and her team at formattedbooks.com were amazing. I am so pleased with the results and the back and front covers.

Elizabeth Schrey for her creativity and tech ability to create my website: kathleen-shea.com

Ginna and David Gordon at Lucky Valley Press have been wonderful to work with in bringing this project to fruition.

For twenty + years I traveled from San Diego to Alaska and would spend two hours a day for a week with students in a gym. I would return yearly, but never got to really know those kids. I remember one time that at the beginning of a new class, a boy in the front row looked up at me and said, "Oh yeah, I remember you. You wore that same green suit last year!"

Then, I had an opportunity to teach seventh grade at Chipman Middle School in Alameda, CA. And I got to know and love those priceless, precious angels and see that the principles of Challenge to Excellence made a positive impression on them. I am eternally grateful to them, and they are the main inspiration for this book.

Of course, I couldn't have accomplished this without the support and encouragement of my husband, Peter and three sons, Stephen, Michael, Peter Ryan for allowing me to tell some of their stories to validate that if they could accomplish their goals so could my students.

This is a family communication workbook to help you through these turbulent years. This is essentially my story and about the importance of God, family, country, realizing your gifts and talents, and achieving your goals.

WRITTEN FOR TEENS AND PARENTS

TO TEENS

You have value. It's not value you earn. Your worth is intrinsic. It's in you, and no one can take it away from you. You are born with this innate characteristic. You are unique and rare. Because of this, you have great value. If you "be the best you can be," then you can achieve your dreams, and the world will be a better place!

There will always be challenges, people who do bad things, adversity, betrayal, and suffering. But you, as a strong individual, have the power within you to overcome these adversities.

I call this book a primer, which just means this is an introduction, a basic book to help you see how valuable you are and to assist you in becoming the best you can be. It is written for a middle school and high school audience. Teens, I am writing to *you* in chapters 1, 2, 3, 4, 5, and 8. Chapters 6 and 7 are written to you and your parents.

Young teens entering middle school especially need to hear this message. You are facing seven of the most challenging years of your life.

Luckily, this book provides a toolbox with some reliable tools to build a strong and resilient self-image. I call it "The Family Survival Toolbox." I know from experience that your parents and high schoolers will need just as much help as you do. The tools I shared for twenty-five years and that I am recommending here have been tried and tested by thousands of students and families.

TO PARENTS

Parents, your greatest gifts to the planet are your children. My firm hope is that at the end of your seven-year journey, the information in these pages will build strong family bonds and enhance and enrich this precious time.

When I look back over my sons' middle school and high school years, as busy and challenging as they were, they remain the happiest years of my life. I look back on that time fondly. I know my sons do too.

I don't want to gloss over how challenging those seven years were. When our sons were teenagers, I was too busy to think about being happy. I was just trying to survive being the mother to three boys all born within three and a half years of each other! My family called them Irish triplets. I certainly did not have all the answers.

When I gave parent talks, I would be introduced as having "three teenage sons and being happily married." I would always respond, "Happily married with three teenage sons is a contradiction in terms!"

When I was a teenager, if my father even looked at me as if he was disappointed, I was devastated. I was a Goody Two-shoes and attended Holy Names Academy in Seattle, an all-girls high school. In my senior year, I was the student body president.

One evening, my husband and I went out to dinner. We arrived home to find that our high school boys had somehow gotten our van stuck in a ditch next to a steep grassy hill in our neighborhood. After we called AAA, we rescued our car, and the boys were asleep, my husband grabbed the car keys.

"I'll be right back," he said.

A few minutes later he walked into our house and put two cases of beer on the island in our kitchen.

Because I was such a Goody Two-shoes, I was astounded.

I asked, "Where did you find that? How did you know you would find beer?"

He looked at me and smiled. "Apple doesn't fall far from the tree."

I can assure you that this Goody Two-shoes would *never* have known there was beer hidden on that steep grassy hill.

When the boys walked into the kitchen for breakfast and saw their two cases of beer on the island, they knew they were in trouble.

My husband just pointed to each one of them.

"You mow the lawn."

"You clean the pool."

"You, get rid of the beer."

"Oh, and you'll all spend a few Friday nights at home."

I am not kidding when I say that these teenage years were some of the most demanding and trying years of my life.

As for my sons, the lessons they had to learn were never easy. Now, thirty years later, our sons are excellent husbands, amazing fathers, and incredible sons.

I can also tell you that I had no idea whether any of these tools would work. Today, I know that the tools you will learn to use in the book not only work but are also invaluable!

There aren't many books written for both teenagers and parents. But I wanted to speak to both groups. A friend who read an earlier version of this book said it was really a "family communication workbook."

If you want to, you can read this book from cover to cover in less than two hours. I recommend that you do read the whole book first before doing the worksheets. It is less than one hundred pages. And at the end of each chapter are worksheets to be completed by the family. This "homework" is essential because it is in the doing and experiencing where the change will take place. I also tell and share stories throughout because examples also help with recalling important concepts.

WHY I WROTE THIS BOOK AND WHO I AM

LIVING MY STORY

Like many of my students, you may think you'll never succeed, but like me, who came from a very humble background, you can overcome difficult circumstances and make your dreams come true. We all have stories, and they need to be shared.

My father's mother died before I was born, and my maternal grandmother died when I was seven. I know hardly anything about either of them. I am the last of my family. There is no one to tell me stories about them. This is true for many of us my age. By the time we are interested in our family history, the people who could recount the stories have all passed away.

When I was four years old, I was visiting my grandparents who lived in Wallville, WA, when someone came to the door and told Grandma that my grandfather, a logger, had been crushed and killed by a falling tree. My first childhood memory is that after hearing the news about my grandpa, my grandma put me behind her kitchen wood stove with a basket of baby chicks and told me to wait there for my aunt.

Grandma came to live with us for a while, and my next memory of her is of the day she died, when I was seven. Recent research has found that the earliest memories tend to be ones filled with emotion, either positive or negative. And both of those negative memories are etched into my brain.

Even if you come from humble beginnings, you can become successful and thrive and flourish. I recently read an excellent book, *Hillbilly Elegy*, in which author J.D. Vance describes his childhood growing up in Ohio and Kentucky. My mother's family were hillbillies, but whereas Vance's mother chose drugs and alcohol and made life miserable and unbearable for J.D., I was more fortunate.

Although my mother grew up poor and often felt inadequate and unsure of herself, she and my dad loved each other, my sister, and me unconditionally. They did this even though life was not always easy, and they always wanted the best for me and my sister.

My parents moved us to Seattle to give us the advantage of growing up in a city and getting an education, one of the keys to achieving the American Dream. I am in awe about this admirable decision to leave everything they knew—their family, their loved ones, their small towns—just to provide us with better education. But despite their courage, I still noticed echoes of my hillbilly past.

When I entered high school at Holy Names Academy, an all-girls high school, my feelings of inadequacy bubbled up, and I immediately knew that I would never be in the "in crowd" unless I denied my past. I came home the first week of school and told my dad that I was going to be the student body president so I could be in the elite group of popular girls. It was a four-year march to attain that goal and to finally be part of the in crowd.

I had the good fortune to have parents, especially my dad, who believed I was just as good as anyone else in school. And now I am sure that one of the reasons he believed that is because Dad was *not* a Hillbilly. He attended Whitman College. He read Shakespeare to us and taught us the Greek alphabet before we knew our ABCs.

But my mother was. When she was ten years old, her family had moved from Missouri to Washington state during the Great Depression so that my grandfather could find work in the logging industry. She grew up in the 1930s on a small farm in southwest Washington state in a house with an outhouse for a bathroom, no hot or cold running water, and no electricity. My grandmother cooked on a wood stove and heated water on the stove to wash clothes and the dishes. As a young child, I remember taking a bath in the kitchen in a big, round metal tub.

My grandfather.

Sometimes when I am taking a nice hot shower and tossing my dirty clothes into the washer and dryer, I think about how my mom grew up. I can't imagine how difficult life was for those early farmers. I can also still picture the dim light of kerosene lanterns in the evenings at my grandparents' home.

When she was eighteen, my mom moved to Seattle and was the companion of a wealthy girl her age and lived in a beautiful neighborhood called Laurelhurst. She went to business school. She could see the University of Washington from her bedroom window, and even though school was free, she said that since no one in her family had ever attended college, it never entered her mind that she could go to college.

There were times when my mother's self-doubt got projected onto me, including when I took my first airplane ride to San Francisco to see Peter Shea after my freshman year in college.

As I was getting on the plane, my mother warned me: "You're stepping out of your class and have no business thinking you could date someone like Peter. He comes from the other side of the tracks."

I was astonished. Because of my dad's positive influence, by the time I graduated from high school, I thought I really was as good as the next person.

Four years later, after Peter and I were married, Peter's mother, Lillian, took me out to lunch to tell me how disappointed she was that Peter married me.

"We had hoped for so much more for him," she said.

Again, I was naively surprised. I told her I was in the who's who of universities and had graduated with honors. My school accomplishments were not what concerned her. She knew, instinctively, that I was a hillbilly.

It was only many years later, after we had a lovely home filled with lovely things, that I could understand why Lillian openly wept at my mother's house devoid of antiques and beautiful things. I didn't agree with the implication, but I did understand and appreciate her anguish.

As if to deny my family history, I scoured the pages of Emily Post's book on etiquette as a young bride, not to only learn how to set the table for my mother-in-law, but also simply to know how to behave correctly. And who gave me that book about the rules of polite society? My mother of course.

But try as I did to rid myself of my past, I came to realize that there is hillbilly still lurking inside of me!

As is true of most hillbilly parents, I never wanted my boys to know what it was like to be poor. I wanted them to be comfortable and feel good in their own skin. I never wanted anyone to laugh at them because they didn't wear the "right" clothes. I never wanted them to be sneered at because they didn't know how to behave in public.

I gave our boys the Nordstrom credit card to buy clothes and always made sure that Christmas was over the top. I made certain that they could go away to college, study abroad, and know that with their gifts and talents they could accomplish whatever they set out to achieve. Because I believed that, they would go on to have all those successes and many more.

Much of this comes thanks to their dad, who is *not* a hillbilly. He provided them with the knowledge, experience, and skills needed to survive and flourish in the business world. At an early age, he made certain that when they met any adult, they had to look them in the eyes, shake their hand, and be able to carry on a conversation.

At a retirement party for Peter's partner, I was sitting with a couple, and when my three boys sat down at our table, the man made a disparaging remark about getting "stuck at the kids' table." By the end of dinner, however, he was amazed at their understanding of the stock exchange, their questions, and their ability to articulate their thoughts.

"We are sitting at the best table," he said at the end of the night.

I just smiled. Probably a very smug smile.

I once told Peter that it could never be said we gave too little to our kids. Quite the contrary, we probably gave them too much. Maybe I did it all not only for my boys but also for myself. I was a hillbilly at heart. Unknown to me consciously, my mom's hillbilly origins and my own feelings of inadequacy still haunted me, which proves that life is an ongoing journey.

HILLBILLY ELEGY

We all have past influences that shape what we believe and who we think we are.

I didn't believe that I was a hillbilly until the summer of 2017. Peter and I were on our way to Oregon, listening to *Hillbilly Elegy* when that realization helped me make sense of certain standout moments in my life. In fact, it made me think about a particularly meaningful moment in my teaching career.

J.D.Vance quotes William J. Wilson's book, *The Truly Disadvantaged*, about black inner-city kids. To me, it seemed that poor white kids and black inner-city kids have a lot in common. As I was listening, a teaching memory poured over me.

I always called my students "priceless, precious angels." One day after school, five or six black kids were hanging around my desk at Chipman Middle School in Alameda, CA, when another girl I didn't know came forward.

I automatically said, "Hi, priceless, precious angel!"

She looked at me, kind of startled.

Regina, sitting at my desk, remarked, "Don't worry. She calls everyone that."

Then another girl looked up at me and said, "You know, Mrs. Shea, you aren't like all of the other white teachers. There's something different about you."

At the time, I just shrugged off her comment, not thinking much about it.

But on that day, listening to *Hillbilly Elegy* in the car, I burst into tears. Peter slowed the car down.

"What's the matter?" he asked. "Are you okay?"

In that instant, I realized what my students, I think, intuitively understood at a gut level: that we all had disadvantages to overcome. We must learn to believe in ourselves. They knew my story about growing up poor, being laughed at, not having the right clothes, and feeling inadequate and insecure.

At the time, I knew how important it was for middle school kids to have adults in their life who could mentor them. I made sure that my classroom was a safe place where they were loved and valued.

I wanted to instill in them the idea that we are each a unique individual. It's not about the group you belong to. It's not about the circumstances in your life.

I wanted them to know that if you changed the thoughts you thought about yourself, worked harder than everyone else, never gave up, and took responsibility for yourself, you could make something of yourself. You might even do great things. We live in a country where all of that is possible.

When I look back on wanting to be in the in crowd in high school and knowing that my only ticket into that crowd was to become the student body president, I see that I was unconsciously trying to overcome my hillbillyness.

It's been said that we teach what we need to learn. What I needed to learn and what I taught was that we are all born with intrinsic value and that with hard work I could overcome my humble beginnings. We all have gifts and talents. We all have our own mission on the planet. These, again, were the primary lessons I wanted to impart to my students and my own children.

CHALLENGE TO EXCELLENCE

I titled my course and this book *Challenge to Excellence*. I didn't call it Challenge to Perfection.

Why? Because the definition of perfection is "free of all flaws or defects," while the definition of excellence is "the quality of being outstanding or extremely good." No one will ever be perfect, but we can all strive for excellence.

I never taught kids to think that they were the best, the greatest, or entitled but rather that they are each endowed with their own individual gifts and talents.

When I taught in Catholic schools, I reminded students that they are made in the image and likeness of God. In public schools, I left out the God part, and I told them to just look at the miracle of how our bodies function. We are individuals, rare and unique, and therefore of great value. With hard work and persistence, my students could succeed.

For me, their eyes were and are the windows to their soul. When I looked into their eyes, I saw something magnificent. We are 100% responsible for who we are. We are also responsible for the good and bad choices we make in our life.

I taught that life is difficult and not always fair. Even when life is unjust and undeserved events occur in our lives, we must get up, dust ourselves off, and get back in the game.

PARENTING

As a parent, you always hope and pray that you did right by your children, that you nurtured them and helped them recognize and use all their gifts and talents. It is a daunting responsibility. One of the first big insights for me was that every child is just who they are, each one so unique and so perfect.

I quickly realized that each of my three boys was completely their own little person. They might be "the Shea Boys," but they have always been as different as night and day!

Often, it is hard to just let go and let them be. You want the absolute best for them, but what is that? I longed for everything in life to be easier for them and superior to what I had. At the same time, I aspired to be as amazing a parent as my mom and dad had been for me. I was loved unconditionally, prodded, encouraged, and expected to behave and succeed. My parents set a high bar for me, one I'll always be grateful for.

I wanted to take what I had been given to another level and be a real advocate for my boys. I made that my mission, my life's work. In the beginning, it wasn't something I could have articulated, but being their advocate took on a life of its own. Then, one day, while teaching *Challenge to Excellence* to a group of teenagers, I called myself an advocate for kids, and a light bulb went off in my head. When I heard those words, I realized that's really what I had become—an advocate—not only for my sons but also for all the kids I was lucky enough to teach. They all became my priceless, precious angels.

I hope my reflections can benefit and support all those who read these stories and complete the exercises to follow.

The only elements of *Challenge to Excellence* that are truly my own are the accounts and reactions of the students, teachers, and parents in my classes.

The foundations at the heart of *Challenge to Excellence*, from goal setting to the affirmations and the visualizations, have all been around forever. This book is, hopefully, an accessible introduction to the world of self-empowerment.

I certainly never maintained that I had all the answers. On the contrary, I always believed that I was gaining as much wisdom and knowledge from my students as they were acquiring from me. It has been gratifying and awe inspiring to know I've had a positive effect on the lives of many of my students.

FAMOUS AMOS

I love the story about Wally Amos, the founder of Famous Amos cookies. Wally Amos was walking on a Hawaiian beach on a day when hundreds of thousands of starfish had washed up on the shore. A young girl was walking toward him. As she approached him, he could see that she was picking up starfish and throwing them back into the ocean.

When he came close to her, he said, "Don't you know that hundreds of thousands of starfish have washed up and you can't possibly make any difference by throwing them back one at a time?"

She looked up at him, bent down, picked up another starfish, and threw it as far as she could back into the ocean.

With great confidence, she replied, "I guess I made a difference to that one!"

I might not have enlightened every single person I encountered, but if I made a difference to at least one person, then teaching *Challenge to Excellence* was a worthwhile endeavor.

APPRECIATIVE

I am also thankful and appreciative for everything I learned from writing *Challenge to Excellence*. This includes the research I did and the other teachers and mentors I learned from, especially Jack Canfield, author of *Chicken Soup for the Soul*. Just after I put my course outline together, I was fortunate to attend and graduate from Jack's Self-Esteem Seminars and later graduate from his Facilitating Skills Seminars.

Everything I taught to teenagers, parents, and teachers for the next thirty years had its beginnings in those powerful seminars. In the beginning, I was honored to be on Jack's Team of Twenty, a group of teachers who were mentored and guided by him. I was privileged to stand in for Jack and to take his place and speak at teacher conferences.

Once, his office called and asked whether I would be willing to fly to Los Angeles and give a talk to 750 high school students. Apparently, according to his assistant, no one in the LA area wanted to take the chance of "being eaten alive by high school kids."

I said, "Sure."

I can remember nervously thinking on the flight that no matter what the outcome would be, it would be a learning experience for me. Far from being eaten alive, I had a great time, the kids were awesome, and I received a standing ovation.

MY FAMILY

Undoubtedly, the most fortunate outcome of writing and teaching *Challenge to Excellence* is that I believe everyone in my own family benefitted from the knowledge and wisdom. My sons did not always greet me with unbridled enthusiasm when I arrived home with a new inspired suggestion for them.

Thank goodness for Peter, my loyal and steadfast husband, who I know for sure was not certain what he was in for either. But he still supported and cheered me on. Together we managed to cajole the boys into trying to achieve some level of competence at setting goals, affirmations, and visualizations. They balked. There was no excitement or eagerness at my suggestions. If it weren't for my husband insisting that they "listen to your mother and do as she says!" I know they would probably have completely ignored me.

MY STUDENTS

When I wrote *Challenge to Excellence,* I had just completed teaching fourth grade at St. Mary's in Walnut Creek, CA. It wasn't until the end of the year when I gave the class a "Who Am I?" essay assignment and the first sentence of the essay started with "I am a marvelous creation, a miracle" that I realized I'd made a big difference in their lives. As anyone who has ever taught knows, teachers always must wait until the end of the year to appreciate all the ups and downs of those nine months and to recognize the influence they have had in their students' lives.

Also, in that fourth-grade classroom, I had a bulletin board with an old Chinese proverb that stated, "Hear and you forget, see and you remember, do and you understand."

That year, we didn't turn to page 56 to *see* the photo of the map of California. We *made* maps of California out of flour and salt so the kids could see and feel the mountain ranges and the big valley in the middle of California.

We studied the California missions from the Native American point of view, and thirty-eight students and eighteen parents spent two days on a Tamales Bay beach *experiencing* what it must have been like being a California Miwok Indian.

I know it was an amazing, unforgettable learning experience for both the students and the parents. I wanted to influence my students to believe in themselves and to be the best they could be.

I would say to my fourth-grade class, "Where are we going?"

And they would say back to me, "To the top!"

I would then repeat in a louder voice, "Where are we going?!"

And they would yell back at me, "To the very top!"

One evening, a boy in my class named Paul was on his way to a free throw contest when he said to his mom, "Mom, where are we going?"

"Paul, we're going to the De La Salle gym for the free-throw contest."

"No, Mom where are we going?"

He kept repeating this question, and finally, very exasperated, she asked, "Paul, where are we going?"

"Mom, we are going to the top!"

Paul won the free throw contest that night.

In 2016, when the Warriors basketball team won their last game, I posted my delight on Facebook, and immediately, two of my former fourth-grade students who I taught thirty-six years ago responded.

Terry: "To the top!"

Shannon: "To the very top!"

I could only smile.

Some of the most heartwarming, gratifying, and encouraging responses have come from my former students.

My students had to memorize a page of affirmations, recite them to me, and write them all down. Then I gave them a laminated copy, hoping it would survive for a few years. Although they might not remember everything I taught them, I hoped that when they read or heard or thought about setting goals, doing affirmations, taking responsibility for their actions, or realizing their gifts and talents, they would recall my class and the lessons we shared.

Ten years after being in my class, my student Tabbitha shared this on Facebook:

> Going through my closet and found this daily affirmation sheet Kathleen Shea gave me back in the day. I swear these daily affirmations always kept me going! I always enjoyed being your priceless, precious angel!

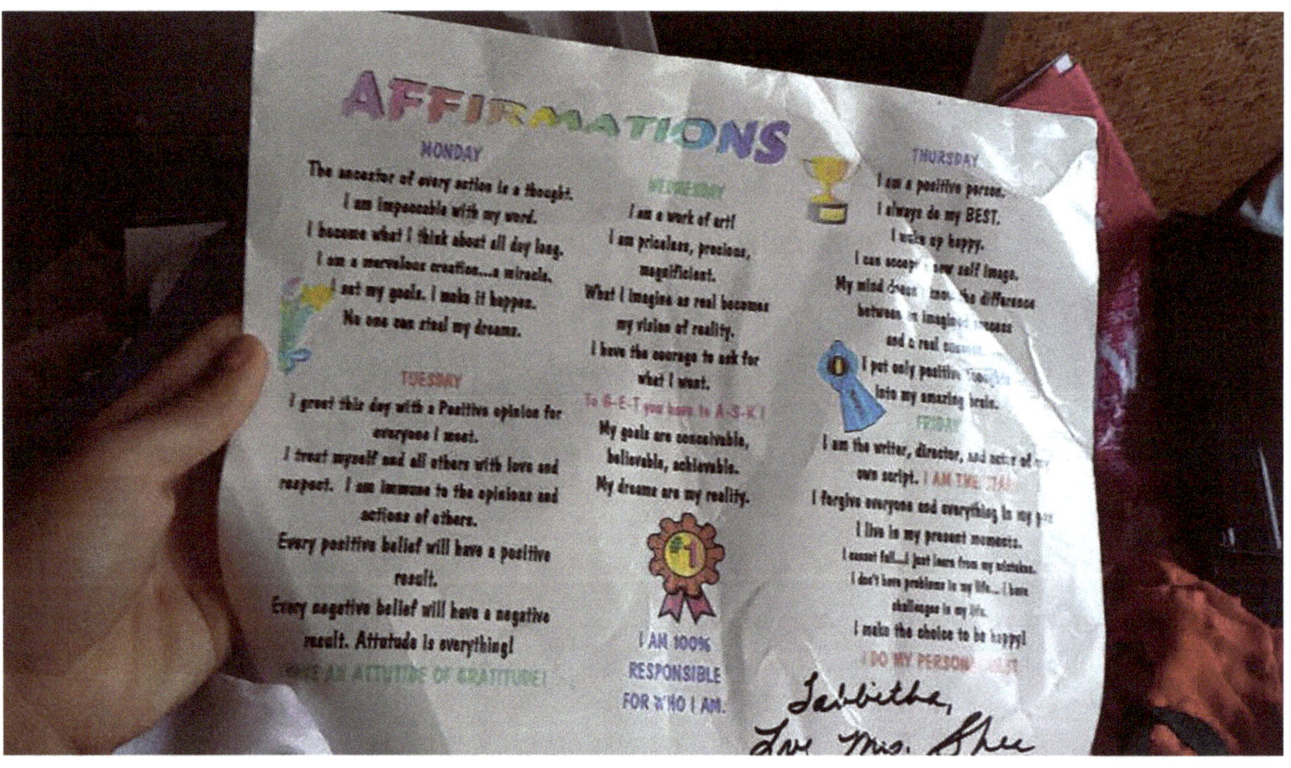

And Tabbitha is definitely a priceless precious angel.

AFFIRMATIONS

This is from another one of my students.

Posted on my Facebook page in 2016 by Jennelle:

> Mrs. Shea, I wanted to tell you a story. So, I walked into what was then Chipman for an interview to become the kindergarten instructional aide and an afterschool program instructor.
>
> They asked me one question.
>
> "Why do you want to work here?"
>
> I burst into tears; at that moment I thought of you. In such a familiar place, I couldn't fight the feelings and emotions I went through as a student in middle school. I finally answered and said to the principal, "I went to school here when I was in middle school; my CORE teacher changed my life and showed me I was worth something. I want to be a constant reminder to these kids that they are worth something too."
>
> 
>
> I wanted to thank you. Every day, in my adult life, I feel I have purpose in helping our youth, to do what was done for me. I have the utmost gratitude for what you did for me over ten years ago. I never forgot. I love you very much.

I taught *Challenge to Excellence* to thousands of middle school and high school kids for thirty years from San Diego to Alaska. And the above quote from Jennelle is the main reason I chose to primarily teach *Challenge to Excellence* to junior high students.

I often saw sixth graders come into junior high confident and happy and then leave eighth grade, three years later, broken, disheartened, and generally discouraged about school.

I wanted to break that cycle. I wanted them to know they were and are intrinsically valuable. Both Tabbitha and Jennelle were my seventh-grade students at Chipman Middle School in Alameda, CA, where I taught for five years.

Seventh grade is probably one of the most difficult years of a preteen's life.

Studies even show that most people were miserable in middle school and hated seventh grade. Once self-assured, happy kids now have new feelings of embarrassment, isolation, and depression because of intense social and academic pressure.

They aren't little kids, and they aren't big kids. They have so many developmental changes happening: cognitive, physical, and emotional with hormones raging. They also think the only ones who understand them are their BFFs, but those BFFs can suddenly turn on them at a moment's notice. This is a crucial time for parental support and clear boundaries.

My passion was to make sure that every student of mine knew I loved them and that they were worthwhile—priceless, precious angels!

There is a quote I heard somewhere that goes something like, "When you are ready, the teacher shows up."

I received a note from a woman in Seattle who wrote and said, "Kathy Shea, you changed my life."

And I wrote back and shared the above quote with her.

I said, "I didn't change your life. I just conveyed some important information, and you decided to act upon it. You are 100% responsible for all the benefits of your actions."

One evening a parent came up to me and said, "Mrs. Shea, I don't know what you said or did, but my son has made a complete turnaround in school. His grades have improved, and his attitude is positive."

I reiterated that quote: "When you're ready, the teacher shows up."

I informed her that unfortunately, not all the kids I taught improved their lives, but I was thrilled to hear about her son's progress.

These two examples remind me that when I was teaching *Challenge to Excellence*, it was as if I was sending a reservation to a celebration, and some people RSVP'd to participate, believe in themselves, and take the necessary actions to accomplish their goals.

When you read these, you can see why I was passionate about teaching teenagers. It took an enormous amount of energy to keep a hundred kids captivated and enthusiastic, but it was hugely satisfying to make a positive difference in their lives.

It's important to see yourself in a positive light.

When people ask what *Challenge to Excellence* was all about, I would show them this photo of a candy bar poster made by students as one of the best and cleverest synopses of my course.

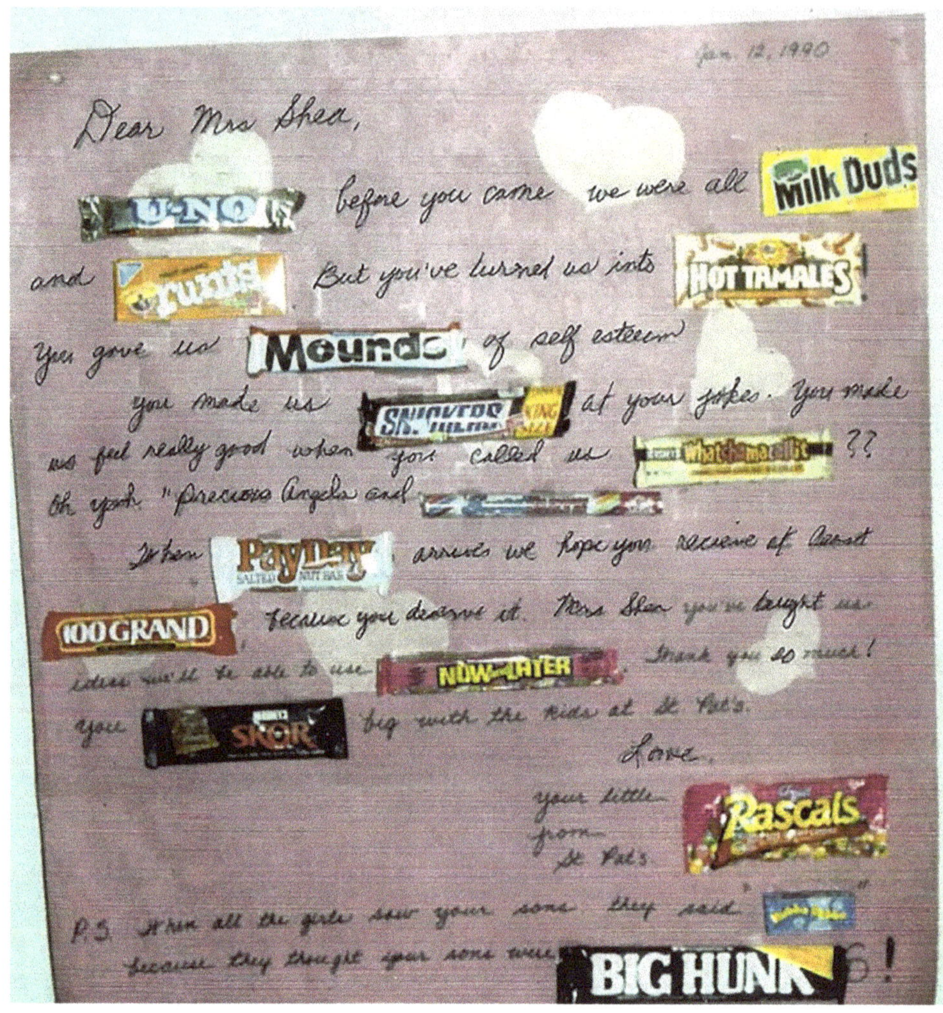

The translation of this poster:

Dear Mrs. Shea,

U-NO before you came, we were all MILK DUDS and RUNTS. But you've turned us into HOT TAMALES. You gave us MOUNDS of self-esteem.

You made us SNICKER at your jokes. You made us feel really good when you call us WHATCHAMACALLIT?? Oh yeah, Precious Angels and SWEETTARTS!

When PAY DAY arrives, we hope you receive at least 100 GRAND because you deserve it. Mrs. Shea, you taught us ideas we will be able to use NOW and LATER. Thank you so much.

You SKOR big with the kids at St. Pats.

Love,
Your little RASCALS from St. Pats.

P.S. When all the girls saw your sons, they said HUBBA BUBBA because they thought your sons were BIG HUNKS!

My main message about my sons, those BIG HUNKS, was that if they could set goals, use visualizations and affirmations, and be double winners, so could my students.

My sons were normal, typical teenagers, not perfect.

You will read stories about how they used these practices and principles to succeed and how they can work for you.

Let's get started.

HOMEWORK FOR TODAY: READ CHAPTER 2.

WHO ARE YOU? A PRICELESS, PRECIOUS ANGEL

Make friends with yourself.

Your self-image is a product of all your past experiences, successes, humiliations, and victories. But it is also influenced by how you think about yourself. You can change your self-image and your outcomes by changing your thoughts. In short, you become what you think about all day long.

Instead of thinking that you're not good enough or doubting your basic worth, try to see yourself in a positive light and make friends with yourself. When you begin to think new thoughts about yourself, you can let that golden inner light shine.

This realization is found in the ancient story of the Golden Buddha.

Many centuries ago, a Thai monastery housed an immense and beautiful golden statue of Buddha. It was over ten feet tall and weighed two and a half tons. After news of an invasion by the Burmese army, the monks sought to protect the statue from thievery and destruction. They  covered the Golden Buddha with several inches of plastered clay, hoping to make it seem like a worthless sculpture that the warriors would have no desire to steal. The monks' noble efforts worked, but they were slaughtered in the raid, leaving the secret of the statue to remain hidden for two hundred years.

In 1957, the monastery was relocated to make room for the construction of a new highway. Its monks arranged for a crane to transport their "clay" Buddha. When the crane began to lift the statue, however, it was much heavier than anticipated—and it began to crack. It also started to rain during this process, and they covered the Buddha with a tarp.

They saw a glimmer of something inside and began to chisel the clay away. At last, the monks came to realize the layers of old, hardened clay were hiding a spectacular golden statue of infinite worth. The statue now resides in the Temple of the Golden Buddha in Bangkok, Thailand, and millions of people visit the magnificent work every year.

We are each like that Golden Buddha. We are golden inside but covered with our betrayals, failures, problems, and worries. Once we become friends with ourselves, we can realize our own uniqueness and understand that we are infinitely worthwhile. We can let our own golden light shine forth.

As a teenager, you also need to be prepared for these tumultuous years!

You need to be strengthened with important information about your teenage years. It's as if you're running a marathon. If you understand and appreciate all the difficulties you will encounter, you can overcome any adversity and be victorious at the end of this seven-year race.

According to the Academy of Child & Adolescent Psychiatry (AACAP):

> Pictures of the brain in action show that adolescents' brains work differently than adults when they make decisions or solve problems. Teens' actions are guided more by the emotional and reactive amygdala and less by the thoughtful, logical frontal cortex.
>
> Adolescents are more likely to act on impulse, misread social clues and emotions, get involved in fights, and engage in dangerous or risky behavior.

Adults think with the rational part of their brain, the prefrontal cortex. This is the part of the brain that responds with good judgment and an awareness of long-term consequences. It is also the part of the brain that helps you regulate your emotions.

Your body and your brain are going through enormous changes right now. The part of your brain that is growing first is the amygdala—the *emotion* area of your brain.

Therefore, you may feel you need more sleep or may often be cranky and impatient. It may also cause emotional outbursts.

During these next few years, you will have all kinds of overwhelming emotions, but your prefrontal cortex—the brain's rational, levelheaded part—is also not yet fully developed. Good judgment is not something you excel in, at least not yet.

It is also important to note that AACAP also says:

> These brain differences don't mean that young people can't make good decisions or tell the difference between right and wrong. It also doesn't mean that they shouldn't be held responsible for their actions. An awareness of these differences can help teens, parents, and teachers to understand and manage their behavior.

It is essential to understand how much your feelings will dominate these important years. Your parents need to be made aware of this too because they are probably wondering, "What happened to my nice, respectful, agreeable child?"

READING A BOOK VS. EXPERIENCING A CLASS

Challenge to Excellence was an *experiential* course. It was based on that line from that two-thousand-year-old Chinese proverb that said, "You do and you understand."

The greatest benefits of *Challenge to Excellence* always happened when the audience or class broke into groups and really experienced the principle I was teaching. It was in the doing and experiencing that the change occurred. That is where all the "Aha's" took place! Again, that is why I will ask you and your family to do some exercises.

Yes, you will have homework.

When you're reading this book, see it as a special time. A time to become friendlier with yourself, to get to know yourself better. Also, let this be a time to look at your friends and family in a new light. Finally, take this time to become friendlier with God.

Most of the time, I taught in Catholic schools where I could say, "You are God's work of art."

But even in public schools, where I left out the God part, I told my students, "You are special, unique, rare, priceless, and magnificent. Because you are rare, you are of great value. No one else in the world has your fingerprints. In fact, your fingerprints can identify you out of the more than seven billion people on the planet. The whorls on your fingers are yours alone. And since each of us is different, we are not in competition with anyone else. We are each in our own league."

When I was teaching *Challenge to Excellence* in the 1990s and early 2000s, a gorgeous woman named Vanna White was on the TV program *Wheel of Fortune*. I would tell my students, "I can't compare myself to Vanna White. I'm not as beautiful as she is, but I have other gifts and talents, and it's my job to improve and use those abilities."

One day, I told this to my class in Palmdale, California. That evening, I was scheduled to give a talk to some of the middle school parents. I found out later that a sixth-grade girl went home and asked, "Dad, are you going to the Parent Talk at school tonight?"

"I don't think so," he replied. "I've had a really long day, and I'm tired."

She said to him, "Well, if you change your mind, tell me if you think Mrs. Shea looks like Vanna White."

When he came to the meeting and told me that he showered, changed his clothes, and came to see if I looked like Vanna White, I laughed out loud!

His daughter had used a brilliant technique to persuade and encourage her dad to attend the parent presentation.

Sometimes I would use this Vanna White story to get more dads to attend my parent meetings. When I saw a lot of dads in the audience and it seemed appropriate, I would "play" that story to the crowd.

I would say, "You don't have to raise your hands, but how many of you showered, changed your clothes, and came to see if I look like Vanna White?"

After lots of laughs and snickers from the dads in the audience, I would say, "I can't compare my looks to Vanna White's looks. I must accept my own gifts and talents. That's what we all must do. That's what your children must do. That's why I'm here. To convince your children that they are worthwhile no matter what they look like. I'm here to convince them of their intrinsic worth."

Out of the more than seven billion people on this planet, no one else has your exact gifts and talents.

When you compare yourself to others, you will always come out better than some and worse than others.

This is often unconscious, but it's important to try to train ourselves to stop. While it may motivate us to better ourselves, constantly comparing ourselves to others can lead to negative thoughts.

For example, when I go to my water aerobics class, I look way better in my bathing suit than some of those other old ladies. But believe me, I also look a lot worse than some of them. None of us look the same.

Another example is how I love to draw. I have drawn pictures of all my grandchildren. However, my drawings cannot compare to the amazing watercolor paintings that my friend Ginny does of her grandchildren.

I just need to be myself. We each have our own gifts and talents. We are all different.

It is also true that we are all alike.

The famous poet Maya Angelou once wrote, "We are more alike, my friends, than we are different."

If someone needs an appendectomy or needs to get their tonsils removed, a surgeon can operate on any human being because our parts are likely to be in the same place.

We each experience challenges, struggles, and victories. We each have our own story. When we tell our stories to each other, we can find common ground.

To build an environment of trust and support at the beginning of each school year, I have my students get into groups of five or six and tell their stories.

I model this by first telling my own story. They each have two minutes to talk about their childhood, their family, their interests, and their hobbies and activities outside of school.

When the first person finishes, the other five take turns and say to him or her, "What I noticed and like about you . . ."

The storyteller would respond, "How perceptive of you to notice, and another wonderful thing about me is . . ."

They take turns until all six have told their story and received praise.

After this exercise I ask, "How do you feel about your group?"

Kids say,

"I know them better."

"Feel closer . . ."

"We are alike and different."

"I found out things I didn't know."

"I feel like we are friends now . . ."

I tell them that I want a classroom where we know and like each other, where we don't compare ourselves, and where it is safe to take risks.

It is true that it is easier and more comfortable to hang out with people who are like us because we feel secure and safe. But when we stretch out of our comfort zones, meet people, and discover how we are different, we have an opportunity to grow.

In school, you can decide to appreciate both kids who are like you and those who are different.

Children often think they need to be like everyone else, which can make them unhappy.

As I said earlier, I always told my students, "Your eyes are the window to your soul. And when I look into them, I see someone with incredible potential and possibilities. You haven't even touched the surface of what you could become."

Life is not fair, and it is not easy. It is challenging at best and sometimes even cruel and brutal. You will have to face all kinds of problems as you grow up. And that is why you must have a strong foundation and be convinced of your own essence, your own goodness.

When you believe in yourself, become friends with yourself, stop comparing yourself to others, and are *strong* at your core, you will know that you are a priceless, precious, and powerful miracle.

I have taught thousands of kids, from San Diego to Alaska, in middle and high school. As I said earlier, the major reason I focused most of my work on sixth, seventh, and eighth graders was because I so often saw sixth graders come into middle school happy and sure of themselves but leave for high school broken and devoid of self-confidence.

My intention was to create an atmosphere of acceptance and respect for each other.

Middle school kids can be mean and ruthless.

Words can be destructive to a person without a strong sense of self. It is imperative that you believe in yourself.

Kids were cruel and unkind long before social media.

I remember when a new girl entered my class about one week into school. She was tall and big, not fat, just bigger than all the other kids.

Someone immediately gave her the nickname "Grisley."

During yard duty, I saw that she was not included and stood alone, looking dejected.

I asked her what she liked and what she was good at.

She answered, "Soccer, basketball, and piano."

I asked, "Would you ever want to play piano for the class?"

She answered, "Sure."

As homework, I told the kids to bring some symbols of success to class.

The next day, when it was Grisley's turn to share, she impressed the class with a huge bag full of soccer and basketball trophies.

I had also rolled a piano into the class. She asked to play. She began by beautifully playing classical music and then amazed the kids with popular present-day songs.

When she finished and stood to take a bow, the whole class gave her a rousing standing ovation.

She looked over at me with a big smile.

Subsequently, she was chosen first for every team. We also had the piano rolled in quite a few times because the kids begged her to play for us.

By the end of the year, she told me she considered "Grisley" a compliment.

Not too long ago, a young friend of mine was excited and looking forward to his first school dance. He was new to middle school, and when he got home that evening, after the event, he told his mom he'd had a great time. The next morning, he received a text from a girl classmate that read, "I just want you to know that I only danced with you last night because I felt sorry for you."

He was deflated, sad, and confused.

Peer acceptance is extremely important for teenagers. It is easy to get caught up counting "likes" on social media. Teens can end up taking hundreds of photos, searching for the one that people will like most. And if the likes don't come in, it can feel very personal.

The other big danger that comes from kids communicating more indirectly is that it has gotten easier to be cruel.

"Kids text all sorts of things that you would never in a million years contemplate saying to anyone's face," says Donna Wick, EdD, a clinical and developmental psychologist. She notes that this seems to be especially true of girls, who typically don't like to disagree with each other in "real life."

I want you to become impervious to what other people think of and say about you. I know you can master this because I have heard from many of my former students, and they attest to the value of the principles you will learn here.

What are your gifts and talents?

Not just what you like to do but what you are good at.

What comes easy for you?

What are some skills you have?

Take some time to think about it.

Take a few minutes to write down your gifts and talents. There are no limits to what you can do; success or failure begins with belief. Therefore, it is necessary to take a good look at yourself in a positive manner. Think about your strengths. What do you like to do, and what you are good at?

What are some things you are good at?

1. ____

2. ____

3. ____

4. ____

What do you put your energy into?

1. ____

2. ____

3. ____

4. ____

What are your strengths . . . your good qualities?

1. ____

2. ____

3. ____

4. ____

What do you LIKE, LOVE, ADMIRE, and RESPECT about yourself?

LIKE – Something you find agreeable, enjoyable, or satisfactory.
LOVE – An intense feeling. A great interest and pleasure. Be fond of.
ADMIRE – Approval. Something regarded as impressive.
RESPECT – High regard. Look up to. Appreciate.

Examples:

1. Things I *like* about myself. <u>I am a good cook, and I have a sense of humor. I like to do water aerobics.</u>

2. Things I *love* about myself. <u>I am caring, friendly, and honest. I love to read.</u>

3. What I *admire* about myself. <u>I always put my family first.</u>

4. What I *respect* about myself. <u>I am a hard worker; I make sure I get the job done.</u>

Your Turn:

1. I LIKE: ____

2. I LOVE: ____

3. I ADMIRE: ____

4. I RESPECT: ____

My Family
What I Like, Love, Admire, and Respect!

FAMILY MEMBER: _______________________

(MAKE ENOUGH COPIES FOR EACH PERSON IN YOUR FAMILY.
HELP ALL CHILDREN COMPLETE THIS, THEN
SHARE OUT LOUD WITH EVERYONE.)

NAME:____

I like about you: _______________________   I love about you: _______________________

I admire about you: _______________________   I respect about you: _______________________

NAME:____

I like about you: _______________________   I love about you: _______________________

I admire about you: _______________________   I respect about you: _______________________

NAME:____

I like about you: _______________________   I love about you: _______________________

I admire about you: _______________________   I respect about you: _______________________

NAME:____

I like about you: _______________________   I love about you: _______________________

I admire about you: _______________________   I respect about you: _______________________

ANOTHER WAY TO MAKE FRIENDS WITH YOURSELF

I sometimes asked my students to make me a list of what they thought their failures were, what they felt guilty about, and what kind of betrayals they had experienced. Then I would stuff small lunch bags with paper. After taking those lists, on the outside of each bag, I would write one failure. Then I took out a huge trash bag labeled "BETRAYAL, FAILURE, GUILT."

Next, I would invite a student to the front of the class to hold the trash bag open for me as I took one lunch bag at a time, read each bag, and dropped it into the trash bag.

"This is the time I flunked my math test."

"This is the time I missed the free throw, and we lost the game."

"This is the time I stole a candy bar and got caught."

"This is the time the girl/boy I liked dumped me."

"This is the time my mother yelled at me again."

"This is the time my parents got a divorce."

I would toss each of these small bags into the trash bag until it was full.

Then I would have the student holding that huge bag of betrayal, failure, and guilt try to sit at their desk and take a test.

Imagine holding it while trying to make a free throw shot or hit a baseball or run a race. How could you even give your mom a hug? They could see how all this betrayal, failure, and guilt was getting in the way of accomplishing their goals.

I would ask, "What can you do with this huge bag?"

The answer is, "You can just put it down."

That is called forgiveness.

When we respond by forgiving ourselves and others, we have the power to produce good outcomes. We have the power to let our light shine. We have the power to be like the Golden Buddha.

We need to learn to forgive ourselves and others so we can stay in the present moment. We know the past is over and there's nothing we can do to change it. The future has not happened yet, and there's no use worrying about it.

Give yourself the gift of forgiveness (make enough copies for each family member).

There is no such thing as failure, only results.
To fail is just to begin again.
Forgiveness is powerful!
I choose to put down my bag of failure, guilt, and betrayal.
I choose to live in the present moment.
I choose to forgive myself and others.

I forgive myself for:

1. ____

2. ____

3. ____

4. ____

I forgive ______________________ for: ______________________

I forgive ______________________ for: ______________________

I forgive ______________________ for: ______________________

I change at my own speed.
Winners are friends with failure. Winners have stick-to-it-ness.

We all make lots of good and bad choices in our life. Some choices are irrelevant. Some are life changing. Here's a fact you won't like: the rational part of a teen's brain is not fully developed until the age of twenty-five.

According to a study from the University of Rochester in New York: "Recent research has found that adult and teen brains work differently."

Adults think with the prefrontal cortex, the brain's rational part. This is the part of the brain that responds to situations with good judgment and an awareness of long-term consequences. Teens process information with the amygdala. This is the emotional part.

That is why you experience your feelings so intensely and may not think through the choices you make and what the long-term consequences are.

You don't want to make choices that you'll regret for the rest of your life—choices about sex, drugs, alcohol, or lifestyle. Before you make critical choices, talk it over with an adult, preferably your parents.

When I was eighteen years old, I made a lifestyle mistake. Of course, at that time, my dad didn't know about the above brain study, but he did know that kids can make decisions based on emotion rather than the possible consequences.

I had just graduated from high school when I came home with papers for my dad to sign so that I could enter the order of the Maryknoll Missionary Sisters. At eighteen, I did not just want to join an *ordinary, conventional* order of nuns. I wanted to travel the world and devote my life to poor children.

My dad might have said, "Are you crazy?"

"What a terrible idea! I don't want you to live so far away."

"This is not the lifestyle I want for you."

But he did not say any of those things. Instead, he said, "I think that's a wonderful idea."

"I'm so proud that you want to live your life for others. But would you do me a favor? Just go to one year of college, and then we can have this conversation again next June."

My Dad had always given me good advice, so I agreed.

After that one year in college, I forgot all about the Maryknoll Sisters. It was not until years later that I asked my dad, "What if June arrived, and I still wanted to be a Maryknoll Missionary?"

"I probably would have asked for one more year," he replied, "but if I thought you were serious, I would have given you my blessing. You seemed more in love with the emotional idea of being a missionary, but you really didn't grasp the magnitude of that decision."

My incredibly wise dad was so right!

Now I'm not saying there's anything wrong with being a Maryknoll missionary. I'm just saying that at age eighteen, I was basing my decision on emotions. I certainly wasn't thinking about the long-term consequences of this choice.

Please take that emotional brain of yours, sit down, and think logically and realistically about how you want your life to look right now and for the next few years. Just because something feels good, does not mean it is in your best interests.

Treat yourself like the priceless, precious, rare, and unique human being you are. Be that Golden Buddha and let your light shine. You have a lot of work to do to develop all your skills and talents.

There are five particularly important truths about human nature that you need to know. I learned these from Grace Pilon, who has a method called Workshop Way.

Grace Pilon says, "It is an educational system for human growth . . . Where we create an environment of security. Where it is okay to make mistakes and not know some particular fact, even at the same time the teacher teaches it and other students know it."

She also says that in our classrooms students should have "an experience of self-esteem and dignity, the bedrock of the growth-through-education process."

She tells her students:

1. "Everyone in this room is smart."
2. "We all learn in our own ways by our own time clocks."
3. "It is intelligent to ask for help. No one needs to do it all alone."
4. "It takes courage to be willing to risk."
5. "It's okay to make mistakes; that's the way we learn."

Read those five truths again. Imprint them in your brain. These truths are brilliant!

Mrs. Shea

You are priceless, precious, unique – a marvelous creation!

NAME______________________________________

FIVE TRUTHS ABOUT HUMAN NATURE

> ### TRUTH # 1
> **EVERYONE IN THIS ROOM IS SMART.**

> ### TRUTH # 2
> **WE ALL LEARN IN OUR OWN WAYS BY OUR OWN TIME CLOCKS.**

> ### TRUTH # 3
> **IT IS INTELLIGENT TO ASK FOR HELP. NO ONE NEEDS TO DO IT ALL ALONE.**

> ### TRUTH # 4
> **IT TAKES COURAGE TO BE WILLING TO RISK.**

> ### TRUTH #5
> **IT'S OK TO MAKE MISTAKES. THAT'S THE WAY WE LEARN!**

1. <u>Everyone in this room is smart.</u>
2. <u>We all learn in our own ways by our own time clocks.</u>

Just because the teacher has a lesson plan that says to teach multiplication on Tuesday, that doesn't mean your brain is ready to learn it. When students know this, it reduces feelings of frustration, anxiety, and boredom that students struggle with. Also, it reminds them that they know how they learn best and that it's okay to go at their own pace.

We all learn differently. Did you know that researchers say there are between three and eight styles of learning? What kind of learner are you?

a. *Visual learner.* These learners need to see pictures. They often like to doodle and draw. They typically would rather see a movie about a topic than just listen to a lecture. They have a good spatial sense for things like maps and almost never get lost.

b. *Auditory learner.* Most musicians are auditory learners. They often like to listen to background music while studying and can typically remember songs. They like to use clever rhymes to help them remember things.

c. *Verbal learner.* These learners prefer to learn through spoken instruction and writing. They typically enjoy public speaking, writing, journalism, and debate. They are often good storytellers. They like to take notes and talk about concepts. They usually have a strong vocabulary.

d. *Physical, kinesthetic learner.* These students prefer to learn by doing, by physically engaging with the materials of the subject matter. They like to get their hands dirty, and they are usually energetic, action oriented, and outgoing. They often like sports and exercise and may seem like they are in constant motion. Careers include emergency services, physical education, and sports.

e. *Logical, mathematical learner.* They are good with numbers. They like any type of learning that logically explains the subject. These learners like to know the reason behind what they are learning. They are drawn to engineering, mathematics, science, research, programming, and other pattern-oriented careers.

f. *Social learners.* These learners like to collaborate and work in groups. They are usually extroverted, good communicators, sensitive, and empathetic. They can fit in with all the learning types because social interaction is what helps them learn.

g. *Solitary learners.* These learners like to work alone and think independently. They can be visual, auditory physical, verbal, or logical learners. They are private. They tend toward careers as researchers, writers and authors, programmers, and coders. They might sit silently in the back of the classroom yet ace the exam at the end of the semester.

I *love* this quote from Albert Einstein: "Everyone is a genius. But if you judge a fish on its ability to climb a tree, it will live its whole life believing it is stupid."

3. <u>It's intelligent to ask for help.</u>
   a. No one needs to do it all alone. That's what the teacher is getting paid for.
   b. You might even need a tutor to help you with a subject you are having trouble with.
   c. If you don't understand, just ask. To G-E-T you have to A-S-K.

4. <u>It takes courage to be willing to risk.</u>
   a. Even something as simple as speaking in front of the class might be problematic for you. The teacher tells the class that even if you give a wrong answer, they will support you because you had the courage to risk being wrong.

5. <u>It's okay to make mistakes; that's the way we learn.</u>
   a. It's better to do things and be wrong sometimes than to do nothing at all.
   b. We all make mistakes, even our teachers and parents.

Again, you have a lot of work to do to find out what your gifts and talents are and what you are good at. Then you must develop those gifts and talents.

Please go to my website kathleen-shea.com
to make extra copies of handouts and worksheets.

DOUBLE WINNERS

I learned about being a double winner from Denis Waitley, a motivational speaker and author. Denis asserts, "If I am worth the effort to be better than I am, and if I make sure that I'm helping other people achieve their goals—that's a double winner . . . If I help you, then I win too."

"When I treat everyone the way I think they want to be treated to feel their best and what will elevate their own feeling of self-worth, we are all winners."

"I'm as good as the best, but no better than the rest."

This is not always easy to accomplish. Trying to become a double winner can sometimes feel overwhelming.

If you are a double winner, you don't mind sharing. You can give without thinking about getting anything in return. Double winners aren't concerned with what they want and need but get all that because they let go of it.

How does that work?

One example is how I have all this information contained in my *Challenge to Excellence* course. I can use it to live a better life or share it with my husband and kids so our family can benefit. But what happens when I share this information with everyone who reads this book? Do I lose it? No. Is there less of it for me? No. In fact, by reaching out to you, something else happens: it multiplies.

You might think, "I don't have a course. What do I have to share?"

How about something as simple as a smile? If I only smile at myself in the mirror every morning, all that happens is some exercise for my facial muscles. If I smile at you, I don't lose my smile. You smile back. Through giving, something is gained.

How about something as simple as a text? We hear about the hurtful effects of negative texts, but why can't your texts to friends look like this?

Let me tell you a story about my youngest son, Peter. This happened during Peter's senior year at De La Salle high school.

My boys played football for Coach Bob Ladouceur, who had one of the longest winning streaks—151 games. Yes, much of it was due to practice and weight training, but Coach Lad always said their real secret was that the team loved each other, that they were committed to each other.

Lad said it was important to share their emotions "because we want those kids to know that there are people there who support them and will always be there for them, that it's a safe environment."

When Peter began his senior year, he was on his way to having an outstanding season. But during the first game, he suffered a hairline fracture in his leg. He was able to play, but it slowed him down and ruined his chances for any accolades.

One evening, at a team dinner, Pete broke down and cried and shared his disappointment that he wouldn't be able to be at his best for the team. On the way home, when he related what happened, I said, "The same thing may have happened to other players this week, but almost certainly none of them had a coach who made it possible for guys to feel comfortable crying and sharing how they felt with their teammates."

After the season, on a warm spring afternoon, Peter showed up at our house with almost the whole De La Salle football team to hang out and swim in the pool.

I was busy in the kitchen when one of the boys came into the kitchen to talk to me.

"I don't recognize you," I said to him. "What position do you play on the team?"

"I'm not on the team," he said, "but your son Pete is responsible for me having the best year of my life."

I was a little speechless but replied, "How in the world did he do that?"

"Well, back in September, I was sitting on the school steps, crying, and Pete stopped and asked me why. I told him I didn't have any friends and I hated school.

"Pete told me to stand up and go to class and that he was my friend.

"When Pete tells you to do something, you do it!

"He also told me that there would be a party after the football game and to come and tell whoever answered the door that I was Pete Shea's friend. After the game, I was extremely nervous, but I went to the party.

"When I knocked on the door, the guy said I couldn't come in. So I told him I was Pete's friend. The guy yelled at Pete, and he yelled back, 'He's my friend. Let him in!'

"I had a great time that night, and after a while, all these guys finally accepted me. Pete really did become my friend."

I was overwhelmed but held back my tears.

When I spoke to Peter later and asked what made him stop when he saw the boy crying, he said, "I guess because I was feeling so down about my broken leg, I thought that could be me."

Then he paused and said, "Maybe I didn't think anything. I just didn't like seeing him sitting there, crying."

This story didn't surprise me; Pete has always been extremely strong at his core. And because he believed in himself, because he knew he was worthwhile, he could be that double winner and extend that same confidence to those around him.

Right now, are there people in your life that you have been mean to or ignored? How often are you mean to a brother or sister? You might be the smartest, best-looking, richest kid in your class or neighborhood, but if you don't make others feel like winners, you are not a winner either.

I want you to be like Pete and make sure that people around you are having the best year of their lives.

Because of his hard work and dedication to the team, his teammates did honor him with the Most Valuable Player Trophy.

The team's motto that year was "Leave No Doubt," and their team started the second streak for De La Salle that year, which led to a historic thirteen-year run of consecutive wins.

TO WIN :
take the
TALENTS
GOD GAVE YOU,
DEVELOP them
WORK on them
and HELP others
at the
same time!

If you want to make change occur in your life, use this simple formula that Jack Canfield taught me and stop blaming events, circumstances, and people.

Events are the things that happen to you.
Circumstances are the conditions of your life.
People are those people in your life.
Instead, focus on your response to those things. That's where you get the power to produce the outcome you want!

EVENT + RESPONSE = OUTCOME

E + R = O

**TO MAKE CHANGE HAPPEN
IN YOUR LIFE
STOP BLAMING:
EVENTS
CIRCUMSTANCES
PEOPLE.

FOCUS ON YOUR
RESPONSE.
THAT'S WHERE THE POWER
IS TO PRODUCE
GOOD OUTCOMES!**

Roger Crawford is someone who was dealt very unfair circumstances in life. He was born with one finger on one hand and a finger and thumb on the other hand. He was also missing his left leg below the knee and had to wear a prosthetic leg.

Yet he didn't go around saying, "I've been dealt an impossible circumstance. I'll never be able to accomplish anything."

Instead, he became ranked as an NCAA tennis player. He put a hole in the bottom of his tennis racket and bounced the ball off the racket to serve. In fact, he was the first and only person in American history to be a United States Professional Tennis Association athlete and play a Division I college sport with a severe disability.

"Lots of people knock having a positive attitude," he once said. "They say it doesn't always work. And that's true; you can have a positive attitude, and things won't work out. But just know this: a negative attitude works all the time!"

Roger Crawford was a linebacker on his high school football team. He said his greatest day was when he intercepted a pass and scored a touchdown. He was on the six yard line when someone tackled him so hard that they grabbed his left prosthetic leg and pulled it off. He made a huge lunge and dove over the goal line.

He said the absolute best part was when he looked back and saw the shocked expression of the guy who was holding his leg!

Roger's parents always told him, "You don't live in Pity City."

"Take your hands out of your pockets, put a smile on your face, go out and do what you *can* do."

"Nobody can do everything well. Go out and do it!"

Roger summed it all up: "I have everything I need to play sports except fingers and legs. The only difference between you and me is that you can see my handicap and I can't see yours!"

"Have I shed a few tears? Have I wished at times that my hands and legs were different? Sure. But all of us go through experiences like this. Whenever we face something in life that looks like a tremendous obstacle, there is always tremendous opportunity."

Roger further explained, "We all have handicaps. I learned what I can't do, like type and eat with chopsticks. Most importantly, I learned what I can do, then I do what I can do with all my *heart*!"

Today, Roger is a motivational speaker, an author, and still a certified tennis professional. His life is a powerful story about how to eliminate excuses.

Focus on your response and achieve more than you think is possible.

We are so fortunate to live in a country where our founders declared in our Declaration of Independence that "We hold these truths to be self-evident, that all men are created equal, that we are endowed by our Creator with certain unalienable Rights, that among these are Life, Liberty and the pursuit of Happiness."

It is not about the *group* we belong to. As an *individual*, you are special, unique, rare, priceless, and magnificent. Because you are rare, you are of great value. You need to know the history of our great country.

I recently met an Iranian man who immigrated to the US twenty-five years ago. When I asked him why he came here he said, "For freedom."

He told me that he was of the Baha'i Faith, which is the second-largest religion in Iran after Islam. He said that after school, he and his brother would run home because they got beat up almost every day.

What he appreciates most about America is that no one cares what religion he practices. He arrived here with twenty dollars in his pocket, and now he owns a grocery store, and his two children are in college. He loves America and says that he is living the American Dream. We take that freedom for granted.

I'm not saying that we must leave our culture and traditions behind.

When I was growing up, my Irish father taught us Irish songs. He often sang "I'll Take You Home Again, Kathleen" to me. My sister and I loved doing the Irish Jig. St. Patrick's Day was a big day in our house. All we knew about my mother's side of the family was that she was from Missouri.

In college, I was a French major. I loved the French language and had an affinity for all things French. Right after Peter and I were married, I was in a souvenir shop to buy a plaque with our Irish Crests. I looked up on the wall and saw one with my mother's maiden name: Garoutte. I said aloud, "Garoutte, that's my mom's maiden name."

The man behind the counter said, "Ah, yes, Garoutte, a fine French name."

I was astounded. French?! I was French? I was a French major. I loved all things French, and I was French? When I told my mom, she didn't know she was French.

A few years later, one of my aunts gave me a book about the Garouttes. It turned out that my great, great, great grandfather, Michael Garoutte, who was related to King Louis XVI of France and a good friend of Lafayette, brought two ships to America to help us defeat the English in the Revolutionary War.

It appears that I am not just a hillbilly but related to royalty!

I wonder what my grandfather Houston Garoutte's reaction would have been had he known his great, great grandfather was royalty!

You may have heard of Lafayette. Lafayette was a French general who played an important part during the Revolutionary War. He helped the colonists against the British. He volunteered his time and money to help the Americans. He was able to help the Americans win the war and was treated like a hero.

At that time in history, no other country's government was "of the people, for the people, and by the people." We were the first free country in the whole of history. That was and always will be an incredible victory for humanity. It is why everyone wants to come to the USA. For freedom.

Lafayette's famous quote: "Humanity has won its battle. Liberty now has a country."

Don't get me wrong. Our country isn't faultless, but it is important to view history through the eyes of our ancestors and what the world looked like to them. Remember that most people 250 years ago couldn't read. Also, the amount of information they were aware of during their entire lifetime would be the same as what we read in the Sunday edition of the New York Times.

They didn't have the advantage of our long view of history.

What makes our country so unique and so strong is that we all come from somewhere else. But when you move to America, you can become an American.

I have seen this in my own family. Our son Michael married a girl from Russia. She recently told me that in all her world travels, the United States was the one country where she was really accepted and welcomed and felt like she was home.

Kristina is proud of her Russian heritage. Our five- and eight-year-old grandchildren speak English and fluent Russian. They know songs and stories in both languages. She keeps her Russian language and traditions alive, but now, first and foremost, she is an American citizen.

Her parents are now here and on their way to becoming citizens. They lived with us for a year. When they first arrived, I asked Irina whether she wanted to stay here and become an American.

She responded in broken English, "Of course, this is Disneyland."

Again, we don't realize how good we have it here.

In 1962, when John F. Kennedy was running for president, I was attending an all-girls Catholic high school. My Irish Catholic relatives were ecstatic. At the time, there was a huge anti-Catholic backlash. People thought that if Kennedy won the election, the Pope would be running the country. If you were a Catholic, no matter what party you belonged to, you voted for JFK.

My dad's overjoyed comment was, "Only in America!"

In 2008, when Barack Obama was elected President, I knew that this was a much bigger accomplishment than JFK's victory. I had a small idea of what every black American must be feeling on that night. We finally did it! I felt pride and elation that at last a black American had been elected to the highest office in the land!

And I knew that somewhere my dad was saying, "Only in America!"

Our country is not perfect. But on that night, I felt genuinely grateful for our Founding Fathers because it really is true that in America: "All men are created equal, we are endowed by our Creator with certain unalienable Rights, that among these are Life, Liberty and the Pursuit of Happiness."

We can rise above all adversity and accomplish our dreams.

On this last Fourth of July, my seven-year-old granddaughter, dressed in red, white, and blue said to me, "Gramma, I'm Irish, and I'm Russian, but most of all, I'm American!"

Life isn't easy. It can be difficult, and life isn't always fair. Some of us are smarter, better looking, great athletes. Some of us grow up poor with lots of disadvantages. Don't play the "victim card."

In America, nothing holds you back from realizing all your potential. Focus on your *response* and achieve more than you think is possible.

Events just are what they are! Response creates outcome.

NAME______________________________________

$$E + R = O$$
$$EVENT + RESPONSE = OUTCOME$$

Write down an EVENT in your life: ____

____

What was your RESPONSE? ____

____

What was the OUTCOME? ____

____

Change your RESPONSE:____

____

How might the OUTCOME be different? ______________________________________

____

We have no power over the EVENTS in our lives.
We do have power over the RESPONSES in our lives, and that makes all the difference in our OUTCOMES.

"NO ONE
CAN MAKE YOU FEEL
INFERIOR
WITHOUT YOUR CONSENT."

"THERE ARE NO MEANINFUL
EVENTS... WE ARE ALWAYS
THE ONES WHO MAKE THE
MEANING."

When you believe the above quote, you are no longer at the mercy of bullies and their mean, disparaging remarks. You know who you are and that you are worthwhile.

Now you have a choice about your response to whatever happens to you. For example, you can go to the breakfast table and be a total grouch, yell at your little brother, tell your **mom** you hate pancakes, and stomp out of the house.

Or you can change your response. You can go to the breakfast table, smile at your little brother, tell your mom that she's a great cook, and go to school looking forward to a happy day.

It's your choice.

You can have it any way you want to.

When you change your response, you change your attitude.

What happens when you get to school and realize you forgot your homework, which gets the teacher upset with you? Again, you have a choice. Your response can be to get depressed, feel terrible about yourself, and beat yourself up: "I'm so stupid! Why do I always do things like this?"

Or you can change your response to: "I'm one hundred percent responsible for my actions," "I make mistakes—that's how I learn, and I'm okay," or "It's not like me to forget my homework."

It's all about your *response*.

In your life, you will make poor choices, but sometimes life-changing, catastrophic events will happen to you that are not your fault and that seem totally overwhelming. That is when it takes all your strength to respond positively. When you are first dealt a devastating setback, it can seem impossible to ever benefit from it.

Such an event happened to me in 2001. At that time, my husband and I were living in Alameda, California, in a nice condo on the water. We were enjoying life, sailing, traveling, substitute teaching, and looking forward to our first grandchild. My husband owned a business on the Pacific Coast Stock Exchange, and his clients were large New York firms.

When the 9/11 terrorist attack happened in New York City, our lives changed forever. We lost friends and business partners that day and were forced to close his company on September 30, 2001.

Peter said to me, "If you want to keep this condo on the water, you will have to go back to teaching full-time."

I was enjoying my life.

The last thing I wanted to do was work full-time again.

I didn't know it, but this was to be one of the best things to happen to me.

I was fortunate to be hired to teach seventh grade at Chipman Middle School. The principal, Laurie McLachlan Fry, was an extraordinary leader of an amazing, skilled faculty. I was given an opportunity to incorporate all the principles from *Challenge to Excellence* into my daily lessons.

When I arrived Chipman had a student body of seven hundred with twenty-six languages spoken.

In 2001, 50% of kids were not reading at grade level.

By 2003, just 12% were below grade level, a drop attributed to an intense instruction program to accelerate students' reading and writing skills. Truly incredible teachers changed kids' lives by teaching them to read so they could excel in school.

In 2005, First Lady Laura Bush—a former teacher and librarian and an advocate for literacy—visited Chipman and paid tribute to our students and our incredible faculty.

"All of us are grateful for all that you do to help our sons and daughters succeed," she told us. "Here at Chipman, you are preparing students for a lifetime of success."

Laurie, our principal said, "The value of this visit is that people who work hard are being acknowledged."

Because my students had written books, she visited my classroom also. It was an honor to receive her approval.

Mrs. Bush had the White House photographer take this photo of Xavier,
Amber, and I and then sent us each a personalized, signed copy.

It also was a reminder that good things can come from what seems like a devastating event. Teaching seventh grade after being out of the classroom for twenty years was not easy.

There were days when I had no idea whether I was making a difference, days when I had to "walk my talk" and show up and do my best.

Mrs. Bush's visit was certainly a highlight, but the very best outcome for me was that those five years teaching at Chipman gave me the incredible opportunity to get to know and love my students and to realize how valuable the practices and principles of *Challenge to Excellence* were to those precious angels.

Ten years later, Xavier responded, "Mrs. Shea!!! I've thought about you so much these past years! I'm so happy for you, and I know your book is amazing, and of course you can use that picture.

"It was one of the best days of my life right there! Your encouraging words got me through so many difficult times in my life. You have no clue the positive impact you had and still have on my life."

Sometimes it takes a very long time before you get validation for your hard work.

Homework:

1. Event + Response
2. Grateful page – do and discuss with family.

REMEMBER: You remember 10% of what you HEAR.

50% of what you SEE.

90% of what you Do.

You need to EXPERIENCE to make it real for you.

Please go to my website kathleen-shea.com
to make extra copies of handouts and worksheets.

What Am I Grateful For?

The world is so full of a number of things,
I'm sure we should all be as happy as Kings.
"Happy Thought" by Robert Louis Stevenson

One way to stay healthy is to write down all the things you are grateful for.

"I am grateful that I was born in America. I am grateful for the freedom we have in this country to pursue our dreams. I must live to my highest potential. I am grateful for trees, flowers, sunshine, rain, clouds, and blue sky. I am grateful for mountains, forests, oceans, lions, tigers, dogs, and cats. I am grateful that I have a place to live. I am grateful for my family, for God, for my health, and for my friends."

Make enough copies for your family, then everyone writes down what they are grateful for.

GOAL SETTING

A goal must be:

- *Conceivable.* You must be able to think it up, to *conceive* of it.
- *Believable.* Other people might not believe you can accomplish your goal, but you must believe that you can.
- *Achievable.* Your goal must be something that you can accomplish. And you just might need to take baby steps to get there.

When our son, Michael, was in eighth grade, he was the class president and the student body president. He had the lead role in the eighth-grade class musical, was one of the stars on the basketball team, and always got A's and B's in school.

Everyone had high hopes for Mike when he went to high school, but something went wrong. First, all his good friends started playing football and were too busy to include him in their group. Next, he didn't study much. Third, he "fell in love" and spent way too much time on the phone. Finally, he broke his wrist during Christmas vacation, which ended his basketball career.

Things improved in his sophomore year when he turned out for football. The coaches saw real talent but a lack of desire. By the end of his junior year, his grades were low, and his coaches called to tell us they were not sure whether Mike would be back for his senior year. They said that usually when they saw kids in a downward spiral, the chances of them making a comeback were doubtful. They really wanted to give him another chance and wondered whether we could do anything to turn his attitude and grades around.

We grounded him and took away the phone.

Most importantly, we sat down with him and tried to convince him that if he wanted to have a great senior year, he was going to have to make some big changes in his attitude and actions. He was going to have to set some realistic goals. Ones he could believe in. Did he have the motivation, timeframe, skills, and abilities to accomplish his goals?

Finally, we told Mike that this was his choice and that he was 100% responsible for the mess he was in. He was also 100% responsible for his comeback if that was what he wanted.

Not too much later, he came to us and said that he was determined to turn his life around and that he needed to set some goals. To do this, he knew that he had to take action but in small steps. He needed to go to summer school, and he needed to run and lift weights every day.

Because one of his goals was to improve his grade point average, he also said he wanted to be tested to see how he learned. That was a huge awakening because he found out that he was a visual learner. He could not just sit in class and listen.

He had to take notes.

He had to draw out the plays in football to learn them.

He had to see what he was learning.

He gave up his summer job, gave up his girlfriend, gave up his summer vacation, and worked his tail off.

Every week, he revised and restated his goals.

He finished the summer with a 3.0 grade point average and was in the best shape of his life.

At the end of the first semester of his senior year, he had a 3.3 grade point average and was the starting strong safety on the football team. His team went all the way to the state finals, and he referred to his last game as "the game of his life."

"DLS SHEA SAVES BEST FOR LAST" was the headline in the paper on the night his team won the championship 41–6. At the end of the season, he was recruited to play college football. None of this would have happened if he hadn't taken 100% responsibility for making a comeback. None of this would have happened if he hadn't set his goals.

His goals were:

- *Conceivable.* He was able to think it possible.
- *Believable.* His parents and coaches might not have believed, but he believed. He knew he had set realistic goals for himself.
- *Achievable.* He had done well in school in junior high. He loved football and knew that with practice, he could become better and stronger. When he was tested and discovered that he was a visual learner, he took notes in class and drew out all the football plays so he could *see* them.

Toward the end of the season, his coach used him as an example to younger kids of someone who turned his life around by setting goals and putting in a lot of hard work.

If Mike can set goals and take the actions to make them come true, so can you!

That's a triumphant expression!

De La Salle's Shea saved best for last

By Alex Valdez
Staff writer

OAKLAND — De La Salle High strong safety Mike Shea was counting on a little motivation from his coaches entering Saturday night's North Coast Section/Reebok 3-A championship football game against James Logan.

"At the beginning of the week, they were saying I needed to have the biggest game of my life," said Shea, moments after the Spartans dismantled James Logan, 41-6, at the Oakland Coliseum.

"And I want to say, it is," he added. "I mean, to have this kind of game in the (Oakland) Coliseum . . . it's great."

Shea, a 5-foot-11, 170-pound senior, collected two interceptions, including a big one that snuffed a James Logan threat late in the first half. He nearly finished with three, but just missed flagging down a pass by quarterback Rick Edwards at the Colts' 40.

> "We kind of got on him and some other guys all week. We told them they had to have great games. Shea really did."
>
> — Luke Werzel

"What can I say?," he smiled. "I almost had that one."

Still, Shea's first interception proved to be one of the key plays of the night. It dashed Logan's hopes of establishing any type of momentum after threatening to cut De La Salle's 14-point lead by six.

"We kind of got on him and some other guys all week," confessed one of De La Salle's defensive coaches, Luke Werzel. "We told them they had to have great games. Shea really did."

Shea did have a little help of course.

After spotting De La Salle a 0-0 lead, Logan finally got on the board with 5:19 left in the first half to make it 20-6.

The Colts forced De La Salle to punt moments later and gained deal field position at their own 47. Logan eventually drove to the Spartans' 5, but a fumble on a pitch-out and Shea's pick killed the drive.

With Edwards looking for Jason Terrell in the end zone, De La Salle's Matt Clizbe deflected it, and Shea was there to make a fine over-the-shoulder grab in the endzone.

"Clizbe made a great play," declared Shea. "He knocked it right into my hands."

Werzel said that particular play was pivotal to De La Salle.

"They (the Colts) were down 22-16 to Pinole Valley after scoring late in the half," said the coach, referring to Logan's 30-22 comeback win in its NCS opener. "That's why that was a big series for us. We didn't want to give them any momentum going into halftime, especially since they would get the ball (to open) the second half."

Shea, though, felt he had to redeem himself after getting burned on Logan's only score.

Shea was unaware that the defense was slated to be in a zone coverage, so he went man-to-man on wide receiver Troy Dominici, who made him pay the price by cutting over the middle.

Dominici hauled in the strike from Edwards and zipped 35 yards for the score.

"I was tired from the big play before (a 34-yard reception by Vince Dueberry)," said Shea, who was a cornerback on the play. "But that play only motivated me more. I looked at every single play more intense. I was hitting harder and reading harder."

Have you ever tried to put together a jigsaw puzzle without looking at the picture on the box? It's almost impossible to do. It's almost impossible to put your life together without seeing the outcome.

That's what happens when you try to put your life together without knowing your goals. You need a destination. If you don't know where you're going, you'll wind up somewhere else instead!

The mind is a powerful tool, and when it has a defined target, it will eventually reach that target. In fact, the mind is like a heat-seeking missile. The missile may not constantly be on course, but it keeps seeking its target until it hits. In other words, when you have a goal, you may not always stay on course, but if you keep persisting, you will eventually reach your goal.

Michael knew where he wanted to be. He persisted and took the actions to make that happen. He accomplished his goals.

"PEOPLE WITH GOALS *succeed* BECAUSE THEY KNOW WHERE THEY ARE GOING."

– Earl Nightingale

Whether you get a ride on a plane, train, bus, or Uber, the drivers know the destination. You both have a goal to arrive at your destination.

You *must* write down what you really want. You must have an action plan.

Goals are life changing and challenging.

If you have no goals and are just going with the flow, you have no destination to reach.

Goals create that big picture for you. They challenge you to be better. Not only do goals excite and motivate you, but you are also satisfied and fulfilled when you accomplish them. You feel triumphant just as Michael felt.

His coaches told him that to win the championship, he was going to have the best game of his life. All his hard work paid off so he could make those two interceptions and help his team win the championship.

GOAL CONTRACT

My Action Plan

I become what I think about all day long.
I am 100% Responsible for who I am.

Name: ______________________________________

My first goal is to: ____

____

What specific actions (choices) will I make to produce the intended results?
ACTIONS / CHOICES:

    1. ____

    2. ____

    3. ____

My second goal is to: ____

____

ACTIONS / CHOICES:

    1. ____

    2. ____

    3. ____

"I__________________________agree to this contract."
    (Sign name)

I have a plan to accomplish my goals.
The only person I can change is myself.

Make enough copies for each family member.

GOAL CONTRACT
For Our Family

*It's a struggle to climb to the top of the mountain,
but the view from the top is magnificent!*

This goal contract is about our family's attitude, faith, values, and traditions. It's about the way we look at life and everything we want for our family. It's about "this is the way we do things in our family; this is what we stand for."

As children in our family, you are loved unconditionally. We love you for who you are, not for how well you do in school or whether you make the team. We want the best for you. We are always here for you.

Life is like a roller coaster. We are all on the same ride, the ups and downs, the good times and bad. How we approach this ride will mean success or failure.

Specifically, the way we approach a job, a class, a paper, a test, a practice, a teacher, a coach, a car, or a friend—in all these cases, it's our attitude, our willingness to work hard, that will make us successful. That doesn't mean we won't ever experience pain or make bad choices, but we are always here for each other.

Our family has a unique cultural and religious heritage, a one-of-a-kind personal identity that we cherish. Our traditions can be generations old, and we can create new traditions that are as simple as a family dinner. Traditions can build lasting memories that give kids the roots of self-development and the wings of self-determination. They help kids know where they come from and where they are going.

Goals for our family can be important, serious, fun, or exciting.

Here are some goals to consider: household chores, game night, family vacation, dinner together, family book club, celebrations, a garden, movie night, a heart talk, or a monthly trip.

Family Goal Contract

1. Goal for our family: ____
    Actions we can take to make that happen:

    1. ____
    2. ____
    3. ____

2. Goal for our family: ____
    Actions we can take to make that happen:

    1. ____
    2. ____
    3. ____

3. Goal for our family: ____
    Actions we can take to make that happen:

    1. ____
    2. ____
    3. ____

Also make a list of traditions and customs your family already has:

1. ____
2. ____
3. ____
4. ____
5. ____

Family Signatures: We agree to this Contract:

____

____

____

VISUALIZATIONS AND AFFIRMATIONS—SEE IT FIRST!

Many well-known athletes talk about being "in the zone."

I am sure you know that countless athletes in all sports have used the powerful tool of visualization. Russel Wilson, Tom Brady, Kobe Bryant, and Michael Jordan are just a few athletes who would first rehearse the game they were going to play in their mind. Jack Nicklaus, a golf champion, wrote a book called *Golf My Way*, and he described visualization as going to the movies:

I never hit a shot, even in practice, without having a very sharp, in-focus of it in my head. It's like a color movie. First, I "see" the ball where I want it to finish, nice and white and sitting up high on the bright green grass.

Is there any science behind visualization? Is it true that your mind can't tell the difference between reality and the thoughts you have?

Srinivasan Pillay says in *The Science of Visualization*:

> Although visualization was regarded as "new age hype" for many years, research has shown that there is a strong scientific basis for how and why visualization works. In other words, we stimulate the same brain regions when we visualize an action as when we actually perform that same action.

The reason visualization works so well is that when people imagine themselves performing flawlessly, they are physically creating nerve patterns in the brain, just as if the body had performed the activity.

Visualization skills are not just for athletes; most people perform in some manner in their daily lives. When you take a test, play a song, or give a presentation, you can create a clear picture in your mind.

Visualization can help you learn a new skill.

Our oldest son, Stephen, loved basketball. Even at an incredibly young age, he had a free throw shot that he could count on. Many times, he made the difference between a win or a loss for his team with his dependable free throw. It was always just there for him.

At De La Salle High School, Steve was the point guard on the varsity basketball team. In his junior year, his free throw disappeared! Obviously, he still had that skill—it was not gone physically. It was gone mentally. The change was all in his head. Around that time, I listened to a tape recording by a sports psychologist who was talking about visualization and the power of our imaginations.

The psychologist said:

> I was being interviewed for a magazine by a disbelieving reporter, and I told him
> to get me any athlete who was having trouble with some part of their game, and
> I know I can get them to make dramatic improvements.

He said that the television just happened to be on, and there on the screen was an NBA player who was having a lot of trouble with his shooting. His name was Byron Scott, and he played for the LA Lakers.

He went on to talk about how he worked with Byron and how much his shot improved. So, of course, I thought, "Wow! This is the perfect tape for Steve to listen to!"

So on a Saturday morning, I snuck into his bedroom and slipped the tape into his stereo. "Just listen to this," I said.

He listened, shrugged his shoulders, and kept having trouble with his shot.

In the meantime, the Lakers were doing well, and Byron Scott was quickly setting the record for being one of the best shooters in the NBA. In 1987–88, Scott enjoyed his best season, leading the NBA champion Lakers in scoring (averaging a career-best 21.7 PPG) and in steals (1.91 SPG).

Byron was the Lakers' starting shooting guard from 1984 until 1993.

Every time he was on TV, Steve would say, "Hey, Mom, there's your man, and he just made another three-pointer."

And I would remind him, "That's because he uses affirmations and visualization."

Finally, Steve made himself a guided visualization tape. He listened to it every night before bed and every morning before he got up. Finally, he believed in himself! Before every free throw, he would take a deep breath and see that shot in his imagination. He would even make a fist and say, "I'm ice!" under his breath.

By the end of his senior year season, he had an 84% foul shooting average.

After his final game as a senior at De La Salle, this headline was in the paper: "SENIOR CASHES IN AT FOUL LINE, SAVES DE LA SALLE WIN!"

The story went on to say,

> In a storybook sendoff, senior Steve Shea was given the task of saving the game for De La Salle in the last home game of his high school career. On the foul line four times in the last two minutes of the game, Shea, who netted 10 points, converted six of seven free throws to give the Spartans a 60-55 win over a scrambling Antioch squad.
>
> "When we needed to hit the free throws, Shea came through," said Spartan Coach George Nessman. "It was his last game here as a senior. And he played like a senior should."

This is another example that shows how you can be a normal kid and still use affirmations and visualization to help you realize your goals.

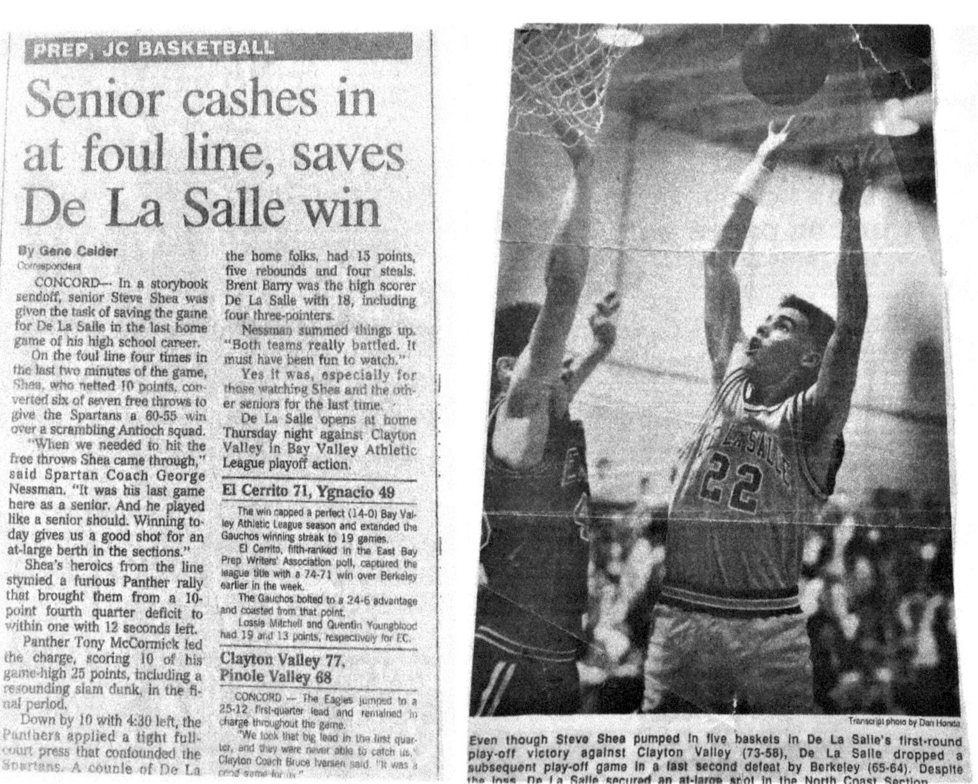

Senior cashes in at foul line, saves De La Salle win

By Gene Calder
Correspondent

CONCORD— In a storybook sendoff, senior Steve Shea was given the task of saving the game for De La Salle in the last home game of his high school career.

On the foul line four times in the last two minutes of the game, Shea, who netted 10 points, converted six of seven free throws to give the Spartans a 60-55 win over a scrambling Antioch squad.

"When we needed to hit the free throws Shea came through," said Spartan Coach George Nessman. "It was his last game here as a senior. And he played like a senior should. Winning today gives us a good shot for an at-large berth in the sections."

Shea's heroics from the line stymied a furious Panther rally that brought them from a 10-point fourth quarter deficit to within one with 12 seconds left.

Panther Tony McCormick led the charge, scoring 10 of his game-high 25 points, including a resounding slam dunk, in the final period.

Down by 10 with 4:30 left, the Panthers applied a tight full-court press that confounded the Spartans. A couple of De La the home folks, had 15 points, five rebounds and four steals. Brent Barry was the high scorer De La Salle with 18, including four three-pointers.

Nessman summed things up. "Both teams really battled. It must have been fun to watch."

Yes it was, especially for those watching Shea and the other seniors for the last time.

De La Salle opens at home Thursday night against Clayton Valley in Bay Valley Athletic League playoff action.

El Cerrito 71, Ygnacio 49

The win capped a perfect (14-0) Bay Valley Athletic League season and extended the Gauchos winning streak to 19 games.

El Cerrito, fifth-ranked in the East Bay Prep Writers' Association poll, captured the league title with a 74-71 win over Berkeley earlier in the week.

The Gauchos bolted to a 24-6 advantage and coasted from that point.

Lossie Mitchell and Quentin Youngblood had 19 and 13 points, respectively for EC.

Clayton Valley 77, Pinole Valley 68

CONCORD — The Eagles jumped to a 25-12 first-quarter lead and remained in charge throughout the game.

"We took that big lead in the first quarter, and they were never able to catch us," Clayton Coach Bruce Iversen said. "It was a good game for us."

Transcript photo by Dan Honda

Even though Steve Shea pumped in five baskets in De La Salle's first-round play-off victory against Clayton Valley (73-58), De La Salle dropped a subsequent play-off game in a last second defeat by Berkeley (65-64). Despite the loss, De La Salle secured an at-large spot in the North Coast Section.

Imagination is a powerful tool. Negative thinking has a negative effect on how we feel and our ability to perform. The images in your mind affect your behavior. Use positive images to empower yourself.

When you use visualization, you create a reality in your mind that is beyond your usual limits by "seeing" it in your imagination.

Tony Robbins, a well-known motivational speaker and author, puts it like this:

Accomplishing goals doesn't start in the physical world—it starts in your head. When you learn to control your emotions and thoughts, you're empowered to accomplish anything.

Visualize the outcome you desire, then think and behave like you've already achieved it. Your actions align with what you want to accomplish, and everything else falls into place. Feel how that success affects every part of your life.

"Whether you think you can or can't you're probably right." —Henry Ford

The Man Who Thinks He Can
By Walter D. Wintle

If you think you are beaten, you are.
If you think you dare not, you don't.
If you'd like to win, but you think you can't.
It's almost certain you won't.

If you think you'll lose, you've lost.
For out in the world, you'll find
Success begins with a person's will.
It's all in the state of mind.

If you think you are outclassed, you are:
You've got to think high to rise.
You've got to be sure of yourself before
You can ever win a prize.

Life's battles don't always go
To the stronger or faster man;
But sooner or later the man who wins
Is the one who thinks they can.

I learned an exercise in guided imagery from Jack Canfield called "The Skyscraper Fantasy."

This exercise demonstrates how powerfully the images in your mind produce physical reactions in your body.

Here is a very short example. See if you can feel the physical reactions when you imagine this:

You are standing in the middle of a very small terrace on the top of the tallest skyscraper. This terrace has no railing. Imagine that you walk to the edge of the terrace. Look down at the street far, far below. Now notice what you are feeling in your body.

Increased heart rate, sweaty palms, shallow breathing dizziness, hollow feeling in the stomach, shakiness.

Return to the middle of the terrace. Open your eyes.

"Where was your body really?"

"In the room, sitting on my chair."

"What was your body responding to?"

"The image I created in my mind."

"Who created that image?"

"I did."

"Who created the experience you had in your body?"

"I did."

Other examples of these kinds of physical reactions could be butterflies before a game, excitement when you think of your girlfriend or boyfriend, or a hollow feeling when you imagine being rejected.

Sometimes we use this mental imagery in a negative way. But we can also use this same skill in a positive way.

Now imagine that you are back on that same terrace, but this time, you can fly! You can imagine that you can fly like Superman or Superwoman, that you have a jet pack, or that you have wings. You walk to the edge of the terrace, push off, and fly. You can fly anywhere you want to go. Spend a minute or two just enjoying yourself.

Now that you have experience creating positive images in your mind, you can use that skill to affect your performance.

POSITIVE IMAGES IN YOUR MINDS ARE CALLED AFFIRMATIONS!

The most important thing about writing affirmations is to write them in the present tense.

Use the two most important words in the English language: "I am."

Your mind does not know the difference between reality and the thoughts you are thinking. "I am a good speller" when you just flunked the test or "I am outgoing" when you are shy may sound like you are lying to yourself, but just remember that your mind cannot tell the difference between reality and your thoughts.

You still must study for the test and go out of your way to be friendly! You must take action to accomplish your goals.

A few examples of affirmations are words and phrases like "excited," "thrilled," "happy," and "having fun."

"I am excited that I am a good speller."

"I am thrilled that I have improved my relationship with my mom."

"I am so happy that I am friendly to all my classmates."

"I am having fun being a more positive person."

Begin by changing the words you say. When you have a negative thought, tell your mind, "Thank you for sharing."

When I first started traveling and teaching *Challenge to Excellence*, I worried constantly. I was worried I'd miss my plane, worried that the school wouldn't have the room set up correctly, worried that I might forget some important part of my talk.

When I conveyed all these worries to Jack Canfield, he did not tell me to stop worrying. He did not tell me to stop thinking about all my worries. Instead, he said, "Kathy, I want you to remove the word worry from your vocabulary for one month. Every time the word worry comes to mind, just tell your mind, 'Thank you for sharing.'"

That seemed easy enough to do, so I tried it for a month. Lo and behold, after those thirty days, I was way less anxious. I had stopped worrying.

If it seems too difficult to change your thoughts, begin by changing the words you say to yourself. Notice how many negative words you use.

Just observe how much better and stronger you feel when you repeat the affirmations at the end of this chapter.

Make it a habit to either read those affirmations or, better yet, say them out loud. Memorize them. Believe them.

Change the words you say about yourself. You don't have to brag, just be positive.

When I first started teaching *Challenge to Excellence* to kids, there were no studies to back me up. Now, there are studies to verify the truth of these principles, and scientists can validate the incredible impact that words and thoughts have on our brain and our ability to achieve our goals.

If highly paid professional athletes use visualizations and affirmations to improve their performance, there is no reason you can't apply this same technique to make your life better.

THE WORDS WE USE USE US

Your words are constantly doing two things: building up or tearing down, healing or destroying.
Every word you speak goes forth from your mouth charged with energy.
Ask yourself: "Are my words alive with life, health, and warmth?"
Choose the words you say.

This is a small list of negative sayings we use and hear all the time:

What a bummer	Makes me sick
Pain in the neck	I'm sick and tired
This cost me an arm and a leg	Dying to meet you
I exploded	I can't see my way clear
I'm starving	I'm on my last leg
I have no idea	My hands are tied
I'll never make it	He bugs me
I'm in the dark	My mind went blank
Spoiled rotten	He erupted like a volcano
I have no desire	Hit me like a ton of bricks
Stick it in your ear	Fell flat on my face
Well, here goes nothing	I just melted
I'm itching to get at	I'm beating my head against a wall
Win a few, lose a few	You could have hit me over the head
Fat chance	Rotten to the core
That makes my blood boil	I could just bite his head off
I'm falling apart	I haven't got a chance in a million
She was crushed	I'm coming apart at the seams
I'd give my right-hand	Kiss you to death
Makes me a nervous wreck	Smother you with love and kisses
Empty heads	This will blow your mind

I cannot stress enough how important it is to change the words you say, to practice setting your goals, visualizing your success, writing affirmations, forgiving yourself and others, keeping a Victory Log, and writing down everything you are grateful for.

The bottom line is that all your negative words and thoughts make you weak. What you put out into the universe, you will get back.

This is so simple to do, but not always easy. I call it "Fake it till you make it!"—to use a classic turn of phrase.

You will have good times and bad times in your life. During those bad times, you must be positive, which can seem practically impossible. When you reach my age, you will be able to fill a book with wonderful, joyful stories and desperate, heartbreaking stories.

Sometimes I look at my life, and it feels like I'm watching a movie. I tell my friends, "You just can't make this stuff up!"

One difficult time in my life was when we had to sell our home. For me, it was a big deal—unexpected and upsetting. Our boys had all gone off to college, and my husband wanted to downsize and make life simpler. I loved our home. We had remodeled it, and I finally had the kitchen of my dreams. I had always thought our grandkids would someday be able to enjoy the backyard and pool.

It felt like I was losing a part of myself, and I was sad for an awfully long time.

Around that time, I had a speaking engagement at a conference in Columbus, Ohio.

Life in Ohio seemed so much simpler to me. One lovely day, the friends I was staying with hosted a barbecue.

I was chatting with a group of people when one fellow turned to us and spoke, "Life just doesn't get any better than this!"

That remark was like a punch to my stomach.

My life felt like it was falling apart.

I found a corner, took a few deep breaths, and regained my composure, but that sadness still followed me for two long years.

I did my affirmations and kept my Victory and Grateful Logs.

We moved to Alameda and lived in a condo on the water. We took up sailing, and life went on.

About five years later, we were sailing on the bay with friends, and there was a gorgeous sunset over San Francisco. Behind us, a magnificent, enormous harvest moon was rising in the east.

We all were in awe. I said to the group, "Life just doesn't get any better than this!" and burst into tears.

All my memories came rushing back.

I was really crying tears of joy because life was better. I realized that if we had stayed in our old home, I wouldn't have made new friends, would never have learned to sail, and—though I didn't know it at the time—would never have gone on to teach at Chipman Middle School.

I've said it before, and I'll say it again. You must make the choice to pick yourself up, dust yourself off, and get back in the game.

This may be a simple concept, but believe me, it's not easy.

Never forget these two big ideas: you will be a success to the degree that you persist, and there is no such thing as failure.

There are only results. You need to separate who you are from what you do!

Never Give Up On Yourself!

Two big ideas:

- There is no such thing as failure.
- You will be a success to the degree that you persist.

Think of some goals you want to accomplish. Write a page of affirmations about those goals.

Begin every affirmation with "I am." Write your affirmations in the present tense because "we stimulate the same brain regions when we visualize an action as when we actually perform that same action." Again, "you become what you think about all day long."

I am excited that I: ____

I am happy that I: ____

I am motivated to: ____

I am thrilled that: ____

I am eager to: ____

I am inspired to: ____

I am determined to: ____

I am delighted to: ____

I am resolved to: ____

Never give up. Most successful people must work hard to accomplish their goals.

Success is not an accident; success is a choice. Stephen Curry, who plays for the Warriors, is one of the best basketball shooters on the planet because he made the choice to create great habits. Your success in life is the sum of the habits you create. If you look at the most successful people in the world, you will see that they have habits that they practice every day.

Make copies for everyone in your family.

When we are in the middle of improving our lives, endeavoring to be more positive, or stretching out of our comfort zones, we need to continue to remind ourselves that we are on the right track. An effective way to do this is to keep a Victory Log. Even the smallest victories are proof that we are making headway.

When we accompany this with gratitude for all the wonderful things in our lives, we become healthier and have more positive attitudes. What we convey to the universe is what we receive.

My Victories. Go ahead and fill pages!

1. ____

2. ____

3. ____

4. ____

5. ____

6. ____

7. ____

8. ____

9. ____

10. ____

Every day at the beginning of class, I would instruct the students to put their heads down and close their eyes. With Baroque classical music (Pachelbel Canon in D) playing in the background, I would ask them to take a deep breath and imagine themselves in a beautiful quiet place.

Then have them: "Repeat these affirmations after me to yourself."

Listening to Baroque classical music in the classroom had a calming quieting effect.

I told my students, "It might not be your music of choice, but it is a tool. It is as if you need a screwdriver (Baroque music), and a hammer won't work for this job."

At the end, it is important to tell them to feel their feet on the floor and their back against the chair as they come back to the room.

Sheila Ostrander, in her book *Super Learning*, points out that with a few minutes a day of Baroque music, classes began to report not only expanded awareness and better memory but also a whole repertoire of health benefits. They felt refreshed, energized, and centered.

Make a copy of affirmations on the next page and memorize.

AFFIRMATIONS

KATHLEEN SHEA

MONDAY

The ancestor of every action
is a thought.
I am impeccable with my word.
I become what I think about
all day long.
I am a marvelous creation ... a miracle.
I set my goals, I make it happen.
No one can steal my dreams.

TUESDAY

I greet this day with a positive opinion
for everyone I meet.
I treat myself and all others with love
and respect. I am immune to the
opinions and actions of others.
Every positive belief will have a
positive result.
Every negative belief will have a
negative result.
Attitude is everything!
I HAVE AN
ATTITUDE OF GRATITUDE!

WEDNESDAY

I am a work of art!
I am priceless, precious,
magnificient.
("A Precious Angel")
What I imagine as real becomes
my vision of reality.
I have the courage to ask for
what I want.
to G-E-T you have to A-S-K!
My goals are conceivable,
believable, achievable.
My dreams are my reality.

I AM 100% RESPONSIBLE
FOR WHO I AM.

THURSDAY

I am a positive person.
I always do my BEST.
I wake up happy.
I can accept a new self image.
My mind doesn't know the
difference between an imagined
success and a real success.
I put only positive thoughts into my
amazing brain.

FRIDAY

I am the write, director, and actor
of my own script.
I AM THE STAR!
I forgive everyone and everything
in my past.
I live in my present moments.
I cannot fail... I just
learn from my mistakes.
I don't have problems in my life,
I have challenges in my life.
I make the choice to be happy!
I DO MY PERSONAL BEST!

NEGATIVE CRITICISM

"Sticks and stones can break my bones, but words will never hurt me."

That old familiar quote might just be one of the most *untrue* statements ever made regarding the consequences of negative criticism and verbal abuse.

I remember, as if it were yesterday, being at my best friend's house when I was about thirteen years old, and her big brother and his friends were having a great old time teasing the two of us.

One gorgeous older boy said to me, "Has anyone ever told you that you are beautiful?"

And I looked up into his big brown eyes and shyly whimpered, "No."

And he smirked and replied, "Well, that's because you are so ugly!"

Then he and his friends guffawed and laughed as I slunk out of the room devastated.

And after that experience, I never, ever believed I was in the least bit attractive. I might not have been gorgeous, but I was not ugly! Thirty to forty years later, I would repeat that story to classes full of teenagers to prove that even after such a long time, that memory was burned into my brain. It had been etched into my psyche. Words can build you up or tear you down.

NEGATIVE CRITICISM PRODUCES A SWATH OF DESTRUCTION

Unfortunately, negative criticism is something that is built into our everyday conversation, especially when talking to our own children. Sometimes, because we disapprove, dislike, are disgusted, are disappointed, or any other "dis" words you can think of, we treat our children to a barrage of scolds and criticism. And the strange thing is that we do this because we love them!

We believe that most criticism is well intentioned. We do not want them to make all the mistakes we have made. We want them to succeed. We tell ourselves it's a very competitive, cutthroat world out there.

"This is constructive criticism; I just want to teach and counsel them."

And so we feel justified. We also don't want them to embarrass us in front of our friends and family.

And most times, our children have heard the same criticisms before.

Think of how often you've said, "If I've told you once, I've told you a thousand times."

Yes, admit it; we've all repeated this to our kids!

I once took a wonderful workshop about negative criticism from Sidney Simon, and he called this the "Red Pencil Mentality." Whatever our kids do, it's not quite good enough.

I'll never forget that when I was in college, my roommate received a letter from home. All excited, she ripped it open only to find the letter she had written home, now filled with red pencil corrections! She never wrote home again.

But here we are as parents, only wanting the best for our children. So how should we react when we are disappointed by, disturbed by, disapprove of, or dislike their behavior? Kids aren't stupid.

After a while, when we ask, "How was school?" or "Was the test difficult?" or "Are you having fun on the soccer team," we get one-word answers. They've learned that if they spill the beans and tell us exactly how they are doing, they will get a blast of criticism. So they opt to just keep quiet.

I passionately believe that if you hope to get through those challenging teenage years and have a great relationship with your children when they're adults, you need to build that foundation of trust when they are very young.

This also builds their confidence and responsibility.

Continue the constant negative criticism at your own peril.

In my experience, constant disapproval, disparagement, and denunciation produce defiant, resentful, and angry teenagers.

Sydney Simon also said we should imagine a gossamer thread between us and the people with whom we are in a relationship. We need to fashion those gossamer threads into steel cables.

The day I took this life-changing class on "Negative Criticism" from Sidney Simon, I arrived home all excited to share everything I had learned with my husband and three teenage sons. The only one home that afternoon was my sixteen-year-old son, Michael.

"Mike," I began to tell him, "I just learned about how destructive negative criticism can be. I am never going to use it again when you boys do something that I am disappointed in, disapprove of, or think is disgusting. I am first going to see if they can pass the Six Filter Test."

In the class, we had to think of six times negative criticism had made our lives better, and I could not think of one time.

"The next time I just want to explode and lambaste you with one of my best scoldings," I continued, "I first have to see if my criticism passes the test of these six filters:

1. Is the person in any shape to receive my criticism? Is he/she hot, tired, and depressed?
2. Do we have time or am I willing to sit down and talk this out—even stay up all night until this is resolved?
3. How many times has this person heard this criticism before? You know, the 'If I've told you once, I've told you a million times!' scenario??
4. Can the person do anything about it right now?
5. Am I positive that none of my own hurts, fears, or mistakes aren't causing me to make this criticism?
6. And finally, am I absolutely positive that this person really needs and will benefit from this criticism?"

As I said earlier, usually when I'd come home from conferences with new information I was met with indifference. Today was different.

Michael exclaimed, "This is just great! I love this stuff."

"And so," I said, "if I can't get through all these filters, I must be a person like Mamie Porter, who was a supervisor of student teachers. And when she would do student-teacher observations, she would not critique her students but sit down after the class and ask these three questions:

1. What did you like about what you did?
2. If you could do it over again, what would you do?
3. And what help do you need from me?"

At this point, Michael raced down the hall to his room and came back with a traffic ticket.

Before I finish this example, allow me to set the scene. At the time, we had two teenage drivers in our family, and our insurance rates were through the ceiling. Besides that, Judge Calhoun at the local traffic court knew me and always smiled down at me from his bench. In his deep resounding voice, he would say, "Well, good morning Mrs. Shea. It's so nice to see you in my courtroom again!"

Whereupon I would take a deep breath, shrug, and try not to show my humiliation to the usually packed courtroom.

So as Michael waved this traffic ticket at me, I was almost speechless. He had me, and he knew it! There were many things I wanted to say to Michael:

"Are you kidding me?"

"What were you thinking?"

"Do you have a brain?"

"You'll never drive again!"

I had been totally caught off guard. It felt like I was mired in quicksand.

So I took a few very deep breaths and between clenched teeth and asked, "Okay, exactly what happened?"

"Well," Mike said, "The other night when I was driving *your* car, I was with Dave, and he had a dozen eggs, and he threw them at a guy in a Mercedes, and the guy called the cops on his cell phone."

Now I really do want to explode! My car! Eggs thrown on someone's car! My kid is no angel, but (in my opinion) Dave was a troublemaker of the first order. I wanted to scream. I stood there shaking my head in complete disbelief!

I thought this was just going to be me sharing my enthusiasm and excitement about everything I learned today. I knew I couldn't stop now. I had to keep going. I gulped and breathed again.

And gritting my teeth again, I asked Michael, "What did you like about what you did, Michael?"

Mike: "I was very polite to the policeman."

Then I asked him, "Did you like anything else?"

Mike: "I got Dave to be polite to the policeman too."

"Then let me ask you this," I said, still gritting my teeth. "If you could do it over differently, what would you do?"

Mike: "I wouldn't let Dave get in the car with the eggs."

I realized that I should keep asking this question until I felt clear.

So, I asked him, "What *else* would you do differently?"

Mike: "I wouldn't hang out with Dave anymore." I'd been trying to tell him that for months!

"Then let me ask you this: What help do you need from me?"

I couldn't believe what he said next.

Mike: "I think I need to spend some Friday nights at home."

This was from a teenager who knew what it meant to be grounded!

After that response, I asked him, "Do you need anything else from me?"

Mike: "I think I need some help with decision-making skills."

Now I was completely astonished, dumbfounded, shocked!

When I asked, "Is there anything else you need?"

Mike responded: "Yes. I need you to go with me to the police tomorrow!"

He'd been holding on to this ticket for a very long time. He didn't want to tell me because he knew the verbal disparagement he would have to endure!

I'm sure by now you're asking, "Well, this is all well and good, but what were the consequences of his actions? Did he have to pay for them?"

Oh, yes, he did. I took him to the police the very next day, and they made him spend a whole day washing police cars. He also stayed home for a few Friday nights. We had some good discussions about his decision-making skills. And finally, he stopped hanging around with Dave.

He took responsibility for his actions.

When it was all said and done, and I recovered from my initial astonishment, I slowly came to realize the simplicity, brilliance, and power of these three questions. In fact, I cannot even begin to tell you how good I felt about that conversation and the resulting consequences. It was the beginning of changing the way I communicated with my sons.

I believe—and I have experienced this with my own sons and thousands of students—that it is vital we keep the lines of communication open. If we want our children to accept the consequences of their actions, we must teach them to be responsible for those actions. They must see that they know:

1. What they did.
2. Why they did it.
3. What other choices were available.
4. How they can learn from this mistake and make more responsible decisions.
5. And that we are here to help them. We are the more resourceful person. We want them to come to us, not their friends, not someone who doesn't have our values.

For them to take ownership of their life, we cannot *tell* them what to do; we need to *lead* them.

Not an easy task! In fact, it is the hardest thing you'll ever do in those preteen and teenage years. No amount of nagging, belittling, ridicule, sarcasm, shaming, punishment, or "I told you so" will get them to change their behavior or help them learn from their mistakes.

To make it last, this change must be their choice.

We must do this over and over and over, day in and day out, month in and month out, year in and year out. It's exhausting. We must create an environment of trust in our homes where we can communicate safely.

When I'm asked, "How do you do that?"

I always answer, "Very carefully!"

The two most important aspects of our communication must be listening and compassion.

Kids learn very early that if they tell us the truth, they, at the very least, are going to get a barrage of negative criticism and/or get in trouble. Now, I'm not saying they don't deserve it, I'm just saying that negative criticism is counterproductive and won't get your child to change his or her behavior.

But most kids will say anything (or nothing) rather than hear:

"You did what?!"

"How could you have been so stupid?"

"If I've told you once, I've told you a million times."

"You didn't study?"

"I told you so."

Be the more resourceful person, the more mature person. You must be that person, not their friends.

The bottom line is that they made a mistake, and what did they learn from it?

I tell kids, "When they make a mistake, there's no such thing as failure. You just get a result. But if you keep repeating that mistake, it will become a failure."

I also told them that if they flunk a test and go home and tell their parents, "This F isn't a failure, it's just a result," don't expect their parents to buy that!

Your son or daughter is going to have to take responsibility for that F and determine what needs to be done to rectify that mistake.

Remember Michael's story, learn from it, and try these questions, which were laminated on our refrigerator:

1. What did you like about what you did?
2. If you could do it over, what would you do differently?
3. What help do you need from me?

The bottom line is that they made a mistake, and they need to learn from it so they don't keep repeating the behavior that got them in trouble. This is always difficult for parents because we certainly don't want them to make all the mistakes we made!

I can guarantee that because these are tumultuous years, your kids will try every patient bone in your body. You will use these questions over and over and over. With some work, you and your child will never feel that sinking feeling that negative criticism causes. You will build those gossamer threads into steel cables. And the best part is that you will revel in the responsibility-building results.

I will also definitely admit that there were times when I *lost* it. I didn't use "The Questions." And there were also times when the boys kept things from us.

Life with teenagers is never perfect, but for the most part, we tried to do away with the criticism and get across to the boys that out in the real world, they were going to have to deal with more than just negative criticism. Teachers will flunk you; coaches will bench you; bosses will fire you. So learn from your mistakes and change your actions to succeed in life.

We have all experienced the demoralizing effects of being criticized, justly or unjustly. Can you just imagine if teachers, coaches, and bosses' husbands and wives asked these questions whenever they wanted different results?

Recently, I asked one of my sons whether he remembered those questions that we had laminated on the refrigerator twenty years ago. He laughed and recited them from memory. Now he's using them with his son and daughter.

Never forget: We must be cycle breakers. Just because we endured negative criticism, doesn't mean that we have to continue that devastating form of communication.

I learned this material from Dr. Sidney B. Simon who, as of printing, is ninety-two years old, living in Florida, and still writing books!

Sidney B. Simon is internationally known for his pioneering work in Values Clarification, now retired as Professor Emeritus from the University of Massachusetts. Over one hundred articles and some thirteen books authored or coauthored came out of that adventurous academic life.

Homework for today: Read this chapter about negative criticism with your family. Discuss new ways of communicating.

Try using the Five Questions on the next page and hang the handout somewhere where everyone can see it.

No matter how we have communicated in the past, we can be cycle breakers!

FIVE QUESTIONS

1. What did you like about what you did?

2. If you could do it over, what would you do differently?

3. What did you LEARN from this?

4. What should your consequenses be?

5. What HELP do you need from ME?

HEART TALKS AND
HEART LISTENING

Heart Talks and Heart Listening is the most important chapter in the book.
I believe that Heart Talks saved my family, and I cannot imagine how families operate without this incredibly valuable tool. You must integrate this practice into your family routine, especially in this age of social media and addiction to iPhones. You will hear me repeatedly tell you that open, honest communication is the key to surviving these tumultuous years.

This chapter is written primarily for parents. It should be read by the whole family.

There is a crisis in our families. We aren't talking to each other! We aren't listening to each other.

If you have a preteen, you are heading into seven challenging years.

You cannot ignore their behavior and just hope that things will improve. They won't get better, and in fact, you'd risk losing your teenager forever.

They are heading into the years when they need to separate from you, but you want that to be a healthy separation, not like so many families today whose adult children have nothing to do with their parents.

Basically, a heart talk is about *listening*. It's about creating a safe space where individuals can be open and honest. Whatever is said cannot be used as a weapon later, and everything said is confidential.

You are the adult in the room. This is your responsibility. I am imploring you to read this chapter with an open mind. I have used this tool with thousands of teenagers and thousands of parents. If you take some time to breathe and think about what you really want for your family, you can successfully use Heart Talks * Heart Listening to heal your family.

At this point, read the Heart Talk * Heart Listening Agreements and read this chapter together.

If you must, give your family a few days to mull all this over before you spring a Heart Talk * Heart Listening session on them.

Don't be surprised at the hurt.

Don't be surprised at the anger.

Don't be surprised that no one in your family, including you, wants to ever do this again! One heart talk won't solve all your problems.

It is the beginning of a long journey.

GENERAL HEART TALK HEART * HEART LISTENING AGREEMENTS

If this feels too long or formal, make your own.

At the very least, read these Heart Talk * Heart Listening Agreements aloud.

This is our family—we are in this together.

1. We agree to support each other in sharing our feelings, knowing that the more we are open and honest, the more authenticity there is in our relationships.
2. We come to this Heart Talk * Heart Listening to heal, not hurt; to keep an open mind and heart, not to judge or condemn; to be vulnerable and open and willing to reveal our deepest feelings, not to name or blame or be right.
3. We come to this Heart Talk * Heart Listening because we love each other.
4. We agree to listen intently with all the love, understanding, and kindness that is available to us.
5. We will create a safe and loving environment in which to share.
6. We respect the sensitivity and privacy of that which is shared, and we will never use what is said as a weapon later.

7. We respect the value of our heart talk and will never violate the confidential nature of what is said.
8. We agree to respect each other's opinions/decisions.
9. We may not agree with everything we each do and all that we each believe, but we all deserve to be heard.
10. Our family goal is to experience all the love, happiness, joy, and enthusiasm that this family deserves.

Believe me, after experiencing this process with my own family, as well as thousands of kids and adults, I know it is vital that you follow the agreements.

Of course, feel free to simplify the language for younger kids.

HEART TALK * HEART LISTENING RULES

Listening with an Open Heart

1. No phones are allowed in the room.
2. Only the person holding the heart can talk. Everyone else must respectfully listen.
3. Talk about how you feel using "I" messages. Stay in the present and come from your heart.
4. Don't dominate the conversation.
5. Don't judge or criticize what anyone else has said.
6. Feel free to pass.
7. Pass the heart to the left.
8. Keep everything that's said confidential.
9. Never use anything said as a weapon after the heart talk.
10. Stay in the group until the heart talk is completed.

Group hug!

As our three sons matured and relationships grew more complicated and competitive, it became apparent that if we wanted to have a close family where everyone was respected and appreciated, we needed to change the way we communicated with each other.

When I first learned about Heart Talks from Jack Canfield, I was teaching my motivational course. As you can imagine, many times my boys were not always thrilled when I came home from another seminar with a new "technique" to try out on the family. I introduced Heart Talks by telling the boys the rules one night at dinner and letting them know we would be having a

Heart Talk at our next family council meeting in seven days. It gave us all time to prepare—and prepare they did!

I told them how much we loved them, that our family came first, that we always needed to be there for each other, and most importantly, that they would be able to unload on Mom and Dad and say whatever they felt with no fear of retribution.

To say that my husband and I were unprepared for the avalanche of hurt feelings and misunderstandings is an understatement! We were also not prepared for how irritated and resentful we both felt. There was nothing easy or enjoyable about that first Heart Talk.

We all survived that Heart Talk * Heart Listening experience, and over the years, these talks became a staple in our family. We used them whenever there was a problem or even for goal setting and vacation planning. We created a safe place for the boys to vent their problems and frustrations with us and each other.

After twenty-five years of open communication and many trials and tribulations, we have kept our family committed to each other. There were times when the difficulties seemed overwhelming, when emotions were raw, when feelings toward each other were bitterly hostile, and when anger and exasperation boiled over. The boys were all born within three and a half years, and they all have huge energy and big personalities. There was always a lot of testosterone in the room!

Our interactions were never perfect, and there was so much exasperation that we never seemed to resolve our problems completely. At this point, I had to convince everyone that just being in a family is a process, that to progress and evolve and grow with each other, we needed this forum to air our frustrations.

We have watched our sons grow into strong, decent men who are not afraid to be open and vulnerable and express their emotions honestly.

In most families and personal relationships, small problems can get blown out of proportion in a short amount of time. Without open, honest communication, barriers are built, feelings get hurt, disrespect occurs, misunderstandings happen, and anger erupts. That's why it is so important that before we sit down to talk, we understand it is imperative to show each other mutual respect and courtesy and remain constructive.

Heart Talk * Heart Listening is the perfect way to implement open communication. We are all looking to be loved and respected. For open communication to happen, we need to stay calm, be patient, show respect, take a positive approach, and focus on *issues* rather than on *individuals*.

Keep the problem and the people separate.

The most significant ingredient in any open communication is how well we listen. Careful listening is giving our full attention, not defending our position.

How often do we mentally prepare our rebuttal while the other person is talking?

Open communication is about opening our ears and our hearts. It is staying focused on the present. While the other person is speaking, we must make eye contact, listen with empathy, walk in their shoes, see their point of view, breathe, and take it in.

I always emphasize how important confidentiality is when engaging in this process. Because of that, it is important for me to say that I have permission to tell you the following anecdote.

My husband recently shared how difficult it was for him to stay in the moment whenever our boys would criticize him. Once, one of the boys broke into tears because he felt wronged.

In his eyes, he was the only one who followed our rules. He wanted his dad to know how angry and offended he felt that his brothers had newer cars and he was given an old junker.

My husband was caught totally off guard and was so overwhelmed by our son's tears and tortured reaction that he had no idea how to respond. He choked up and apologized. Dad's vulnerability was unexpected but appreciated.

I cannot emphasize how difficult but necessary it is to breathe, stay in the present, let go of anger and humiliation, and come from a place of love and acceptance. Believe me, this is one of the smaller confrontations we faced.

When it's your turn to speak, don't defend. Come from a mindset of "This is how I felt when that happened," not "You're a jerk for always being late to the last six lunch dates."

Maintain a theme of "I love you; I just want to spend time with you," or "I feel disrespected, and I want to be part of your life."

Remain flexible: "I know life is hectic."

Agree it's a problem: "Can we find an acceptable solution?"

Brainstorm that solution.

When I did parent workshops, I used a powerful activity to show the importance of listening. I would break the group into pairs (preferably with someone they did not know) and have each pair sit knee to knee and make eye contact.

Each person was given ten minutes to talk *without interruption*.

The other person could only nod and smile.

There was no: "Oh, that happens to me too," or "I know just how you feel," or "Let me tell you about the time that happened in my life."

No, the person just had to listen.

Most often, individuals started out talking about immediate problems: work, the kids, stress. But ten minutes is a long time (uninterrupted!), and by the end of the allotted time, they would be revealing their hopes and dreams, the things that mattered most to them. Many times, the person speaking actually got to the bottom of some of their problems.

What was very profound for me and amazed me the most was that after this activity, people began to treat each other like long-lost friends. Again, it was such a strong validation of how important it is to be listened to!

I also always did this early in the day of my workshop because something else I learned was that most of the people looked like they had a lot on their minds.

Their heads were so full that there was no room for any new information. The same thing happens in our close relationships—our heads are so full of our projections, biases, opinions, judgments, and anger.

When we are given the opportunity to speak freely from our hearts in a completely safe environment, with no fear of retaliation or criticism, and everything we say remains confidential, we are empowered to speak our truth and share our deepest thoughts and feelings.

We are given the chance to open our hearts and create real intimacy and vulnerability in our relationships.

I will never forget the time in San Rafael, California, when I gave a parent talk about the importance of listening and the power of Heart Talks * Heart Listening. The school secretary came up to me the next morning in tears and told me a story about her son, who was a junior in high school and always shrugged her off with responses like "I'm fine, school's okay."

After the parent talk, she arrived home to find her son slouched on the couch. She asked him how things were going. His response was the usual shrug.

She stepped in front of him, handed him a pillow, and said, "As long as you are holding this pillow, I can't interrupt you. No matter what you say, it's confidential, and I can't use what you say later as a weapon."

She could hardly hold back her tears as he confessed that his girlfriend had broken up with him. She wanted to say, "Why that little b—!" but she kept silent.

He went on to tell her that he had flunked his chemistry test. Again, she held her tongue. And finally, the football coach had benched him.

He talked for half an hour. At the end of his confession, he said that he knew breaking up was for the best, that he needed some help with chemistry, and that he was going to make an appointment to see the coach.

She finally asked, "Do you need anything from me?"

"No," he replied, "but it felt great to get all this off my chest. I think I can handle it, but let's do this again."

As he walked to his room, she stood there with her mouth open. She was floored! All she did was keep her mouth shut and listen!

Every time I reread this account, I get choked up. This just confirms the importance of listening to our kids. Sometimes they even have the answers they need if we give them the time and attention to just be there for them.

Another example of the power of Heart Talks * Heart Listening happened when our boys were in high school. My sister, her three boys, and my mom and dad were joining us at our Lake Tahoe house for a week.

Our family was in a complete disintegration mode; no one was getting along. Pete and I had driven up to Tahoe on a Friday ahead of the boys because our oldest son didn't get off work until 10:00 p.m. and the other two had a football game that night.

Pete and I had just fallen asleep when the phone rang and jarred us awake. The boys were yelling on the phone and having a huge argument.

Pete calmly told them, "You all get in that car and drive up the mountain now."

As he turned off the light he said, "We're meeting them at the front door in three hours."

That Heart Talk * Heart Listening encounter lasted from 1:00 a.m. to 6:00 a.m. Five hours of airing their frustrations, calling out the apparent unfairness (in their eyes) of Mom and Dad's rules, and the spilling over of long-held hurts. There were lots of tears, heated debate, misunderstandings resolved, and a bottom-line realization that we loved each other.

And just like at the end of each Heart Talk * Heart Listening, we made a commitment to each other that whatever offense or upset we were responsible for, we would make a valiant effort to mend our ways.

By the time we all crawled into bed for a few hours' sleep before the cousins arrived, it felt like we were whole again. The boys experienced a wonderful week with Grandma, Grandpa, and my sister's boys.

Through the years since, if one of the boys had issues with each other, they would have an individual Heart Talk * Heart Listening, and those remain confidential to this day. The importance of confidentiality cannot be stressed enough.

Today, when I extol the virtues of heart talks to my friends, I am committed to keeping the content of our family heart talks confidential.

When we really listen with an open heart, we get the chance to see love in action, build strong bonds, and be ourselves without fear of retribution.

Many times, when we gathered as a family, the topic of conversation or the situation was uncomfortable, but sooner or later it became unavoidable. It would be so much easier to ignore and act as if it didn't exist. No one wants a heart talk!

It is never easy, but how often is the right thing to do also the easy thing to do? And so we always begin with the agreement to support each other and a review of the rules.

Even if we think there is only one concern or problem, it always turns out that there are multiple issues that need to be aired. After so many years of taking part in this process, I can't imagine how other families function without Heart Talks * Heart Listening.

The boys are now all grown up and have families of their own. They live in different states, and it is rare when we are all together.

We have not gathered for a whole family heart talk for a long time, but since we instituted this tradition, we don't hesitate to voice our concerns with each other whenever we have problems. And I know that if we had a family crisis, we could count on our boys to speak freely and from the heart to help solve any difficulty.

To be honest, I miss those special family-sharing moments with my boys. And I would love to be a fly on the wall when they have their family Heart Talks!

Recently, our youngest son confided to us how important and useful Heart Talks have become with his five-year-old daughter and seven-year-old son. And to show how something so simple can have a huge effect on a child's life and in the steady, reliable functioning of a family, my youngest son Peter related this story to me.

They had been having trouble getting their six-year-old son, Brogan, out the door and on his way to school on time without a lot of daily balking to get ready.

During their, Heart Talk * Heart Listening as Peter's wife, Melanie, began speaking about chores and the importance of everyone sharing the workload. Brogan sat with his eyes looking at the floor.

Next to speak was my son, Peter. He said he thought that Brogan was probably expecting that he would have a similar list of expectations for the kids, but instead he had an issue with his wife. As soon as he began telling Melanie why he was upset with her, Brogan's head snapped up, and there was an expression on his face that said, "Oh, you can really say anything you want during a heart talk!"

So when the heart came to him and it was his turn to speak, he looked at both of them and earnestly said, "I just want to comb my own hair!"

Since that Heart Talk * Heart Listening, the morning routine of getting ready for school has hugely improved because Brogan can now comb his own hair!

The author of Heart Talks, Cliff Durfee, died in October 2014.
I learned about Heart Talks from Jack Canfield.

Cliff's first book was called *Feel Alive with Love, Have a Heart Talk* and was published in 1979. It assists friends, couples, and families in having harmonious and loving relationships. The seven-step Heart Talk went on to become a popular communication technique used in youth groups across the nation. In 2005, a chapter of the book *The Success Principles* was devoted to honoring this technique, which Jack Canfield used in many workshops over the years.

HEART TALK * HEART LISTENING TOPICS

Something I do well is . . .
Something I'm getting better at is . . .
Something I do for Mom is . . .
Something I do for Dad is . . .
I can . . .
I am proud that I . . .
I get people's attention by . . .
I get my way by . . .
My greatest strength is . . .
I can help other people to . . .
I taught someone to . . .
I need help on . . .
I know I can get better at . . .
I'm learning to . . .
When people try to boss me around, I . . .
I don't like people to help me with . . .
Something I can do by myself . . .
I got into trouble when I . . .
The most powerful person I know is . . .
I want to be able to . . .
I'm not afraid to . . .
Something that I can do now that I couldn't do
last year is . . .
I have difficulty dealing with . . .
I have accomplished . . .
If I want to I can . . .
If I were the teacher I would . . .
I do my best work when . . .
I get angry when . . .
When I get angry I . . .
When I feel sad I . . .
When I feel scared, I...
I get scared when . . .

Something I want but I'm afraid to ask for is . . .
I feel brave when . . .
I felt brave when . . .
I love to . . .
I see myself as . . .
Something I do well is . . .
My friends are . . .
I love to . . .
I see myself as . . .
My friends are . . .
What makes me a good friend . . .?
I like people who . . .
My best friend . . .
I wish I had the courage to . . .

These are just a few topics to choose from. They all work and have been used successfully in hundreds of classrooms. Try them, invent new ones, and watch as your children grow to believe in themselves and their ability to achieve their goals.

ADOLESCENCE AND REVIEW OF BIG IDEAS

YOUR CHALLENGE TO EXCELLENCE
IT'S NOT EASY, BUT IT'S POSSIBLE!

Too many kids are unnecessarily broken by adolescence. During these next few years, you need to decide whether you are going to be an "outer" kid or an "inner" kid. To be an inner kid, you must decide to like, love, and admire yourself.

You must be *so* strong that you can face all the social media and peer pressure and remain intact.

No other generation has ever had to face the challenges of social media. We have no idea what the long-term effects are going to be on your age group.

Especially if you are an outer kid, whose self-image is determined by the whim of the latest trend, the opinion of the popular kids, their appearance, and so on.

I want to play a visualization game with you.

So sit back and relax.

Put a picture in your mind of a cute little house, complete with flower boxes in the windows, nice green grass, and a white picket fence. This house is surrounded by tall trees, and it is very shady and cool.

You see yourself opening the gate and walking up the stairs to the front door. You enter this little house and find that it's so small. It's just one room, but what a wonderful room. There's a nice cushy carpet, a fire in the fireplace, comfortable chairs, and lots of neat books and toys that you played with when you were a child.

You stay there for a while but soon realize that you are starting to feel kind of closed in and claustrophobic. You wish there were more rooms in the house and that it was not so small. You are also getting bored with all these kid toys.

You leave the house and walk down the path. As you walk down this shady path, you see that it leads to a sunny meadow. Beyond the meadow is a beautiful river with a bridge crossing it. As you walk toward the bridge, you see a sign that says, "Leaving the Town of Childhood! Hope you enjoyed your visit!"

You keep walking on the path and as you approach the bridge, you see another sign: "Adulthood just seven years down the road. Drive Carefully. Winding road and many bridges are out."

As you look toward the town of Adulthood, you can see that it is huge. The lights are bright, it looks like a wonderful place, and you are excited to get on the road.

Let me explain this visualization.

The nice little house is obviously childhood, where you spent many comfortable, maybe even delightful, years. There was always someone to meet your every need and to put a Band-Aid on your knee when you stumbled and fell.

But you have grown out of childhood, and you can see that there is something better ahead for you: adulthood. You will be on your own. Maybe you will go to college or get a job, travel the world, and have a career. You might get married and have a family. There are all kinds of great adventures waiting for you, but first, you must get through these teenage years.

It is during this time that a few bridges are out. I am here to warn you about those bridges so that you don't drive off them. If you know that some of them are demolished, you can be prepared to just drive around them and get back up on the highway to Adulthood.

Most teenagers drive off some of these ruined bridges.

One ruined bridge is: teens feel inferior.

I recently read an article online and was amazed at the statistics that many teenagers said they felt inferior.

According to a Pew Research Center survey of US teens ages thirteen to seventeen, about three in ten say they feel a lot of pressure to look good (29%) and to fit in socially (28%), while roughly one in five feels similarly pressured to be involved in extracurricular activities and to be good at sports (21% each).

After reading this book, you know this does not make any sense. We are all children of God. We are complete and whole just the way we are.

You do not need to compete with other kids. You can be friends with yourself. You can accept yourself. But so many teenagers decide that they lack dignity and worth. Why do so many teenagers feel this way? Why are they so bitterly disappointed with who they are?

Many teens believe that a winner is good looking, has money, is an athlete, and gets good grades.

A good number of teenagers do not like the way they look.

You spend a great deal of time in front of the mirror with creams and soaps trying to undo all of Mother Nature's damage.

You think you are too short, too tall, too thin, too fat.

Think about people you see when you go to the mall, the grocery store, a sporting event, or a concert.

They wouldn't fill the pages of fashion magazines. Most people are not gorgeous. You think that you will only be successful if you are beautiful or handsome.

This is one of the bridges that are out. It causes so much pain.

We are all beautiful in our own way. We don't need to make the pages of fashion magazines to be successful.

Another bridge that is out is that teenagers feel stupid.

The Pew Research Center also found that when it comes to the pressures teens face, academics tops the list: 61% of teens say they feel a lot of pressure to get good grades.

When kids feel unintelligent, they give up; they quit trying.

But now you know that it is not true. Everyone is smart. There are different styles of learning.

There are lots of examples of brilliant, successful people who had trouble in school:

- Thomas Edison, a brilliant scientist, was thrown out of school at age twelve because he was terrible at math and unable to focus. His teacher said he was too stupid to learn anything.
- Salma Hayek is a Mexican-born actress, producer, and humanitarian activist. She was diagnosed with dyslexia in her teens.
- Danny Glover is a Black actor and political activist. Due to dyslexia, he was once described by a guidance counselor as "retarded."
- Albert Einstein is best known for developing the theory of relativity, but he also made important contributions to the development of the theory of quantum mechanics. He did not speak until he was four and could not read until he was seven years old. One

of his teachers described him as "mentally slow, unsociable, and adrift forever in foolish dreams."

- Magic Johnson, the all-star basketball player, overcame dyslexia and dominated the court as one of professional basketball's best players for thirteen years. His counselor at school advised him to go to summer school, which he did and surpassed.

  "I am not the only one that has a problem. But I didn't let my ego or peer pressure get in my way," he said at a speech at a high school. He didn't let the disapproval and criticism get to him. Instead, he used it as a constant motivation tool to rise above and get where he is today.

  "You're the only one who can make the difference. Whatever your dream is, go for it," he said. He is an astute businessman and a philanthropist. He won many battles before getting to where he is today.

- Winston Churchill, England's famous prime minister, had to repeat a grade in elementary school.

- Steve Jobs, the cofounder of Apple, did not care about school until his fourth-grade teacher bribed him to do his work. She used candy and money as a reward. He was also bullied as a kid.

- Steven Spielberg, an American film director, producer, and screenwriter, dropped out of high school in his sophomore year. He was convinced to return but was put in a "Special Ed" class.

- Walt Disney was fired by a newspaper editor because "he lacked imagination and had no good ideas."

All these people overcame their learning problems and went on to be phenomenally successful. On the other side of the coin, if you have been blessed with high intelligence, if school and learning are easy for you, then much is expected from you.

Another ruined bridge is peer pressure. I call this bridge: virtual peer pressure for this digital generation. Between Snapchat, Instagram, Facebook, and Twitter, most kids spend at least seven hours a day online. Think of it like candy. Some of it is great, but too much of can destroy your health.

The National Center on Addiction and Substance Abuse at Columbia University:

Research now shows that too much time spent in the cyber world is rewiring kids' brains and affecting their ability to succeed in the real world.

Teens today suffer from anxiety, depression, and attention disorders. Just ten years ago, bullies had to torment you face to face. Now hate groups that could ruin your life can be created online behind your back. This study at Columbia University showed that when teens see their friends involved in drugs, sex, and alcohol, 75% of them will replicate that behavior.

We have never faced a ruined bridge like this one. We have no idea what the long-term effects will be on your brains. Tom Kersting, the author of *Disconnected*, maintains that your brains are changing because you are so dependent on the constant stimulation of electronic devices that it can make it almost impossible to concentrate and focus in class.

There are a lot of wonderful features about the access we have to instant information. I love staying in touch with family, friends, and students on Facebook, Snapchat, and Instagram.

However, you owe it to yourself to get educated about the risks and hazards of being so attached to social media and your phone.

Two snippets from the book *Disconnected* that enlightened me:

- The average age of children having a cell phone is getting younger and younger. It's now at ten years and three months.
- School plus technology does not equal smarter students. In fact, it seems like it hinders focus more than it helps.

There's a school in Silicon Valley where 70% of the students are children of "Big Tech" employees, and there isn't a screen in the school. No laptops, no tablets. Kids use their imagination and pen and paper.

The products and apps that the big tech companies create, design, produce, and sell are good enough for the public, yet they actively protect their kids from using them because they know the effects.

I mentioned another broken bridge earlier: the emotional part of your brain. The amygdala is growing and changing faster than at any other time in your life, creating havoc with your feelings and making it difficult for you to make rational levelheaded decisions.

It's as if you are working with a brain that is still under construction.

Sometimes you seem mature, and other times your decisions are illogical and impulsive.

You *feel* more than you *think*. It is important to talk through your decisions and stay connected and involved with your parents. Besides, there are a lot of decisions that you do not need to make until you are an adult. Enjoy being a kid.

No matter what social media or "experts" say, you do not have to make adult decisions when you are a teenager. This time should be about learning about and improving yourself.

That is a big job.

Two of the biggest ideas:

- There is no such thing as failure, only results.
- We keep our lessons, and we learn from them.

When you look at successful people, you may not see their failures.

Abraham Lincoln lost his first congressional race at age thirty-two.

Eight failed races and twenty-eight years later at age sixty, he was finally elected President of the United States.

He did not see those struggles as failures. He persisted; he never gave up.

Mistakes are how we grow, learn, change, and improve.

I make mistakes every day, your teacher makes mistakes, and your parents do not want you to make the mistakes they made.

I would love it if I could give you all the information in *Challenge to Excellence* so you could go out into the world and experience only positive results and make no mistakes. Sadly, that's impossible.

I wrote and taught these principles to make you aware of your own goodness. You are unique and of great value. You are a priceless, precious angel. When bad things happen to you, just stand up tall and repeat to yourself,

"No matter what you say or do to me, I am a special person. I'm a priceless, precious angel."

"You're fat!"

"You're ugly!"

"You have bad breath!"

"Hey brace face!"

"You'll never make it!"

Repeat to yourself: "I'm a special person. I'm a priceless, precious angel!"

In your teenage years, you will do a lot of dumb things. I want you to do little dumb things and learn from them, not big dumb things that are life changing. I used to have two big rules in my family:

1. Do not get killed.
2. Do not kill anyone.

Not long ago, fourteen teenagers were killed in alcohol-related driving accidents near where I lived. That is a dumb mistake that has life-changing results!

I want you to make the choice to feel so good about yourself that you can stay away from peer pressure and avoid getting caught up in the drugs and alcohol culture.

You can be cool and not drink.

You can be cool and get good grades.

You can be cool and be a double winner.

You will be a success to the degree you persist.

Suppose during this time you had a goal. You visualized it. You took action to make it happen. Whether it was to get 100% on a spelling test or to make the basketball team, it did not happen.

Do you give up? No.

Did Steph Curry give up? No.

Did Abraham Lincoln give up? No.

Successful people never give up. Success does not happen immediately.

It takes small steps.

It takes an action plan.

It takes hard work.

It takes enthusiasm and commitment.

An Inspiration

A wonderful lesson of persistence can be found in the story of a young woman named Deshauna Barber. She is an American beauty pageant title holder, a motivational speaker, and a captain in the US Army Reserves. At nineteen years old, she was told that she could be Miss America. She tried and lost six years in a row but finally won the title of Miss USA on her seventh try, in 2016.

"Do not fear failure," she says. "Be terrified of regret."

Her story is one of never giving up.

Deshauna says:

> Many of us have goals we are trying to achieve, but the person we are right now is not the person we need to be when we cross the finish line to our dreams. We must walk and pace ourselves because we haven't grown enough to fit into the shoes we need to achieve our aspirations.

YOU BECOME WHAT YOU THINK ABOUT ALL DAY LONG

The good news is that during this time, you have changed. You will *never* be the same again. The information you have read and experienced here has been programmed into your mind, and it will be there when you need it.

You see yourself differently. You know the truth about you. You know that you are a child of God, a truly marvelous creation—a priceless, precious angel. Because you are unique and rare, you are of great value. You know that you are the most important creative power in your life.

You are responsible for the kind of life you are going to live. You make the choices to determine what kind of person you will be. You decide whether you are an observer or a participator.

You know that life is not easy or fair. You know that suffering and pain are a part of life. When hardships happen, you know that you must dust yourself off, pick yourself up, and get back in the game. You have made friends with yourself and accepted who you are. You have experienced how good it feels to see yourself in a positive light.

You know that your imagination is like a movie preview of life's coming attractions. You choose to change the words you say. You know that negative words and thoughts make you weak. Positive words and thoughts make you strong.

You are one of the successful people who have written goals because you have learned how important it is to record your goals and affirmations.

You know that the two most important words in the English language are "I am." You write your affirmations in the present tense because your mind cannot tell the difference between your thoughts and reality.

It is called "fake it till you make it."

You have experienced forgiving yourself and others, and you live in your present moments. You have memorized the affirmations in this book.

One vital thing to remember is that this is not just a book to read once, put down, and forget. This is a guidebook for you to use often. It's like a good friend who you should visit regularly.

You and your family must make a habit of practicing these principles. They need to become part of your routine. Your teenage years can be exciting, fulfilling, and worthwhile. Think of this time as a rehearsal for adulthood.

How you practice and prepare now will guarantee your success in the future.

Set your goals, visualize, be grateful, and keep your Victory Log.

In ancient times, the map makers wrote, "There be dragons!" on the edge of their maps.

What lies ahead for all of you is unknown. You will face dragons because there is evil in the world. And there will be a lot of dragons you must slay!

Those map makers never wrote, "Beyond this, there be beautiful oceans, vast forests, untold riches, and great opportunities!"

There are definitely risks, danger, and evil, but there are also beautiful oceans, vast forests, untold riches, and great opportunities.

This book is just the tip of the iceberg. It is just a primer course, an introduction to the principles you need to thrive. You have not even tapped into your gifts and talents. It will take a lot of effort on your part to reach your goals.

I challenge you to use this material daily. Epecially in this digital age, it is imperative that you take some time for yourself every day to keep your amazing brain strong and dynamic.

There was a time when you might have been scared to face this unfamiliar time.

Sure, you might be a little nervous, but you are now equipped with a tool bag full of everything you need to drive around the damaged, ruined bridges and arrive at adulthood, complete, whole, and ready to realize your dreams.

The opening credits have started on the film called "Teen Years."

You are not only the writer, director, and actor of your own life movie.

You are the star.

MORE HOMEWORK

On the next page, you will find the Ultimate Affirmation, where you are going to describe yourself as if your life and everything about it is a ten and everything is rewarding.

Describe your appearance, your performance in school, your performance on the basketball court, on the swim team, or at the piano, and all your activities as if all these areas are ideal.

Describe how your life would be if you knew you could not fail.

You do not have to be *perfect* to have a satisfying, fulfilling life.

You just have to do your best.

Also describe your relationship with your friends, parents, teachers, coaches, brothers, sisters, and more. If you think that you do not know how you could possibly describe this wonderful existence, remember that you—and only you—have all the answers.

You may have to look deep inside to find how you would live your life at a ten, but it's your life, and only you know what a ten is for you.

All our answers are inside ourselves. Some people spend their lives looking outside for solutions. They dream about striking it rich, maybe winning the lottery.

Yet all they need to do is look inside to find out they could live a more rewarding life using their own God-given gifts and talents.

I am excited and thrilled for you because I know you have unlimited potential.

If you look at yourself and say, "Are you kidding? I'm not sure I can be a success."

You are saying that because you have a lot of work to do.

It will take a lot of effort on your part to reach your goals.

I won't promise that it will be *easy*.
I promise that it is *possible*!

Make enough copies of the Ultimate Affirmation on the next page for everyone in your family.
Everyone in the family can write their own ultimate affirmation.

Share your affirmation at a Heart Talk * Heart Listening session.

Please go to my website kathleen-shea.com
to make extra copies of handouts and worksheets.

Ultimate Affirmation

NAME ____ DATE ____________________

Write the Ultimate Affirmation: "I AM A STAR."
"I am priceless, precious, magnificent and I am a precious angel."

"I AM excited and thrilled:"

____

____

____

____

____

____

____

____

____

____

To be a star, you must shine your own light and not worry about the darkness because that's when stars shine the brightest!

LETTER FROM THE AUTHOR

Dear Readers,

In the first chapter of this book, I told parents that their children are their greatest gift to the planet. I can confess to you that *Challenge to Excellence* was never financially successful. I almost always worked "outside the system." I do not have a pension. I did not make millions of dollars. Thank goodness for my successful husband.

By many standards, the world would say I'm a failure. I disagree. I have made a difference in the lives of my family and my students. I am not perfect—no one is. But the validation I have received makes my heart sing. I am eternally grateful that I have used my gifts and talents to the best of my ability.

I turned seventy-five this year, and my sons gave me the greatest gift. I told my husband that I did not want a big party but to spend my birthday at the Little River Inn in Mendocino.

The next week, we celebrated with a lovely family party.

I made a beautiful Shutterfly book with the touching texts I received from our sons on the morning of my birthday. Reading those texts, my husband and I shed a few tears.

When you know how much they love and appreciate you, it makes it all worthwhile.

Peter Ryan (youngest son):

> Mom, you taught us the importance of unconditional love, and as a parent, I realize this is the most valuable experience that I can pass on to my kids. Thank you for always being there for all of us. You are the glue that holds us together.

Stephen (oldest son):

> I wanted to thank you for teaching us to love, how to be great parents, and how to always stick together through thick and thin. I feel so blessed to be a part of our incredible journey together as a family. Thanks for all you do, all you have always done for all of us. I love you and want you to know that I appreciate all of your unconditional love.

Michael (middle son):

> Our family's journey together has been an amazing ongoing experience. You and Dad have taught us that, in the end, what is most important is family and our love and support for one another. Life is not supposed to be easy, and God gives you only the challenges you can handle, overcome, and come out the other

side a better person. You and Dad, through all your trials and tribulations, have always displayed a positive and compassionate attitude. Thank you for being a great example.

When I read those texts, I know that my life has been a success for me. This is what I want for you. I want you to experience the joy of knowing that you did what was best for your kids and the people in your life.

I know that if you practice the information in this book, someday, when you are my age, you will be able to look back with great joy and know that your legacy is your talented, beautiful children and that you have made the world a better place.

I am most blessed.

So now it's your turn. And when you are old, you can write your own success story.

Good luck. God bless you, and let me know about your progress.

I would love to hear from you and would appreciate all feedback.

Kathleen Shea sheakath@gmail.com

BIOGRAPHY OF KATHLEEN SHEA

Kathleen Shea is a retired credentialed educator. She wrote and taught a motivational self-esteem course called *Challenge to Excellence* to thousands of junior high and high school students, parents, teachers, student teachers, and administrators. She did this through workshops, weeklong seminars, retreats, and leadership conferences.

She is also a certified teacher of the Enneagram, which she taught in the Come Alive Program at St. Mary's College in Moraga, California.

Her last teaching assignment was teaching seventh grade at Chipman Middle School in Alameda, California. This provided her with the tremendous opportunity to really get to know and love her students and convey the principles of *Challenge to Excellence* daily.

After forty years of making a difference in the lives of others, she now enjoys life with her husband of fifty-five years and loves being the best Gramma she can be to her five grandchildren.

DEDICATION

This book is dedicated to my husband, Peter for his patience and validation and to and our three sons, Stephen, Michael, and Peter Ryan for being willing to apply these concepts in their lives. In our journey as a family, not only have we all benefitted from these principles, but I believe they have saved our family.

I also dedicate this to my seventh-grade students at Chipman Middle School in Alameda CA for the opportunity to get to know and love them and to realize the positive effect the concepts of *Challenge to Excellence* had on these priceless, precious angels.

My gratefulness to them is one of the primary reasons I wrote this book.

Likewise, I dedicate this to my grandchildren and all the students, parents, and teachers I have taught. I believe that it is now time to tell my grandchildren—Kennedy, Brogan, Sierra, Vitaliya, and Sebastian—the story of their Gramma's motivational course, *Challenge to Excellence.*

As the years rush by, I feel an urgency to leave a legacy for these precious angels. I may not be able to bequeath them a monetary fortune, but I am trusting that the wisdom in these pages will enable them to live richer lives. I am hopeful that my enthusiasm for these principles will also become their passion.

I also dedicate this to my sister's grandchildren: Keeley, Raylin, David, Cooper, and Matia. My sister died four years ago from ALS. When I first began teaching *Challenge to Excellence*, she was one of my biggest supporters. I know she would want her grandkids to have this information.

TESTIMONIALS

I had success teaching high school kids, student teachers, teachers, administrators, and parents. I am including some favorable opinions of my course here, but I also want you to know that on a scale of one to ten, I did not always receive tens.

From Joan Davenport, Program Team Leader, School of Education California State University, Hayward:

"All 70 students on our Multiple Subjects Credential Teams have given me such positive feedback about the self-esteem workshop which Kathy conducted for us. I have seen a change in their general attitude; the climate is much more optimistic. Thank you for sharing your knowledge and talent with us. We think you are truly an incredibly special person."

However, one teacher wrote on her evaluation that I was: "One of the most dangerous people on the planet." My boys always thought I should use that quote as the title for my book.

Another incredibly wise person said to me that less complimentary judgments make the positive ones real. Another afterthought is that negative reviews or comments tend to be the ones we remember.

Michael H. Kenney, Bishop of Juneau, Alaska, Sitka Youth Convention:

"I want to express my profound thanks to you for the wonderful work you did with the kids during our Youth Convention. Two things amazed me. First, the immediate and obvious rapport you had with the young people. Second, I was surprised at how much the materials you presented touched the teenagers. I came to appreciate you both as a person and a professional. You bring together, in a wonderful way, trained skills and a loving soul.

MY BROCHURE
(next page)

Quotes From Educators:

Sr. Adrienne Peinnette, O.P., Principal, St. Philip Neri, Alameda, California:

"I am very excited about the program and very grateful that Kathy Shea is taking the time and energy to do something so special with our Junior High students."

Karen Judy, Eighth Grade Teacher, St. Marys, Walnut Creek, California:

Through five superb sessions, "CHALLENGE TO EXCELLENCE: validated the good things I am already trying to communicate to my students, as well as offering fine modeling of overt self esteem building techniques that I tend to overlook or take for granted.

Kris Brown, Principal, Holy Rosary, Seattle, Washington:

Kathy Shea gave so much to all of us: students, staff and parents. Her program enriched our lives. Jesus challenged us to excellence and positive living, and Kathy Shea does the same in a dynamic way. Her time with us was a gift".

Quotes From Parents:

"Not only was Mrs. Shea's presentation to the parents worth while, but what she did for my daughter was even more outstanding. With Kathy's class, Jill has blossomed. She is now anxious to go to school, she is talking with her Dad again and taking an interest in the world around her!"

"We all want our children to grow up to become happy, well balanced adults. Academics are valuable, self-esteem is invaluable. This class for our students was fantastic!"

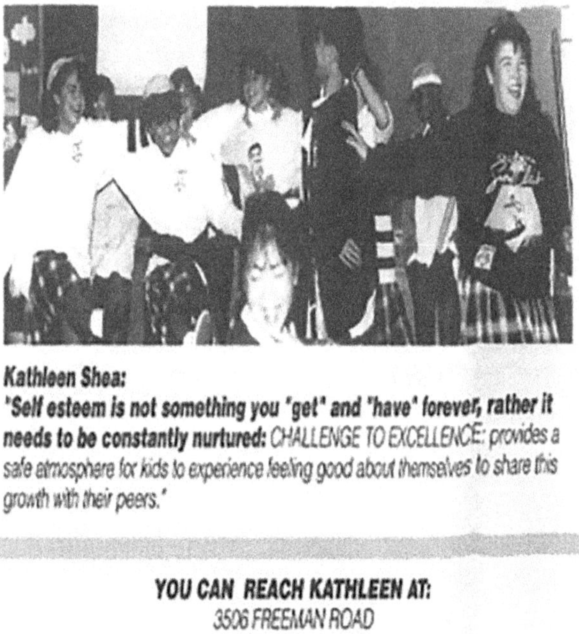

Kathleen Shea:

"Self esteem is not something you "get" and "have" forever, rather it needs to be constantly nurtured: *CHALLENGE TO EXCELLENCE: provides a safe atmosphere for kids to experience feeling good about themselves to share this growth with their peers."*

YOU CAN REACH KATHLEEN AT:

3506 FREEMAN ROAD

WALNUT CREEK, CA 94595

415 946-1428

CHALLENGE TO EXCELLENCE

A SELF ESTEEM COURSE FOR TEENAGERS

"...I LEARNED THAT THERE ARE NO LIMITS TO WHAT I CAN DO..."

Challenge to Excellence

Challenge to Excellence is a program to build awareness and skills in positive thinking, affirmations, self image, and self confidence; setting goals, accepting responsibility, making choices, learning self acceptance, the power of forgiveness and to commit each adolescent to being mentally, spiritually, and physically healthy!

In addition to workshops for adolescents, CHALLENGE TO EXCELLENCE also offers programs for parents and educators.

YOU ARE GOD'S WORK OF ART

Adolescence

Adolescence is a time of change and growth. These crucial years can 'make' or 'break' a child. The seven years it takes to travel from adolescence to adulthood can be a positive, inspirational time or a desparate, demoralizing time.

Your SELF ESTEEM (how you view yourself and your world) will determine the success or failure of this 'trip'.

YOU BECOME WHAT YOU THINK ABOUT ALL DAY LONG!!

What It's All About!

"Thanks for a wonderful time, Mrs. Shea. I learned to believe in myself."

"Before I felt useless, fat, stupid, and about two inches tall! Now I feel like I'm special."

"I let all the bad things pile up. I felt guilty. Now I feel free. I love this feeling. Thank you!"

I hear and I forget.
I see and I remember.
I do and I understand.
Chinese Proverb

Kathleen Shea is the author and President of Challenge to Excellence, a Self Esteem Course of adults and teenagers.

She has been a credentialed elementary and junior high teacher for twenty years.

Kathy currently lectures nationwide.

She has conducted in-service workshops and seminars for 1000's of teachers and parents.

She has touched the lives 1000's of junior high and high school students through week long seminars, retreats, leadership conferences and workshops.

Kathy also works with numerous corporations and has been a consultant to Marriott Hotels/Host International.

Kathy is a graduate of Self Esteem Seminars Facilitating Skills Seminar. She is also a consultant for Jack Canfield's Self Esteem Seminars and she and Jack are co-authoring a book on self esteem for teachers and parents.

She has co-authored and teaches a Spirituality of Self Esteem Course for adults.

Kathy is happily married, has three teenage sons and lives in Walnut Creek, California.